About
Writing
and How
to Publish

Also by Cathy Glass

Cathy Glass

About Writing

and How to Publish

HarperElement
An imprint of HarperCollins*Publishers*
77–85 Fulham Palace Road,
Hammersmith, London W6 8JB

www.harpercollins.co.uk

and HarperElement are trademarks of
HarperCollins*Publishers* Ltd

First published by HarperElement 2013

1 3 5 7 9 10 8 6 4 2

© Cathy Glass 2013

Cathy Glass asserts the moral right to
be identified as the author of this work

A catalogue record of this book
is available from the British Library

ISBN 978-0-00-754221-5

MIX
Paper from
responsible sources
FSC™ C007454

FSC™ is a non-profit international organization established to promote
the responsible management of the world's forests. Products carrying the
FSC label are independently certified to assure customers that they come
from forests that are managed to meet the social, economic and
ecological needs of present and future generations,
and other controlled sources.

Find out more about HarperCollins and the environment at

Acknowledgements

A big thank-you to my readers for insisting that I write this book. It is one I have wanted to write for some years, but it took my readers' encouragement to make me find the time.

My thanks – as always – to my editor Holly, my literary agent Andrew and to Carole, Vicky, Laura, Hannah, Virginia and all the team at HarperCollins. I certainly couldn't have done it without you!

Contents

Introduction

I receive many emails asking for advice on writing, and many of those I've helped have gone on to publish their work. Unfortunately, I don't have the time to help everyone who contacts me asking for advice, so I've written this book, which I think will help all you budding writers. But first, a few words about me – the author.

The Author

I have been a writer for as long as I can remember. To begin with, I published poems and short articles in the school magazine, and also kept a detailed diary. In my teens I progressed to writing short stories, newspaper articles and a few radio plays, and began to enter writing competitions. Then, in my early twenties, I wrote a full-length book. So writing has always been there in my life. However, for me, as for many, it was initially a hobby; something I did in my spare time while I earned a living and then later fitted around being a mother and foster carer. It wasn't until I wrote my first bestseller – an inspirational memoir – that I began to claim time for writing, although even now, seventeen books later, my writing time is still early in the morning so that it doesn't impact on my family commitments. It is also the only time the house is quiet and my thoughts uncluttered. I have three grown-up children, and many of my books have become international bestsellers. For more about me and my work, please visit my website: www.cathyglass.co.uk.

SECTION ONE:
ABOUT WRITING

Why Write?

The simple answer is that you write because you want to; because you have a compulsion, a desire – often a burning desire – to share your thoughts, ideas and experiences through writing. It's like an itch that won't go away and will only be relieved when you put pen to paper or start typing. If you are thinking of writing to make a fortune, forget it. While top journalists and a few bestselling authors make a good living – with a lot of hard graft – from their writing, the majority do not. Less than 1 per cent of published authors earn the minimum wage; that is, enough to live on.

Most authors, therefore, write for reasons other than money – although of course it's nice to be paid, and if you have a piece of work published then you should be paid. With so little chance of receiving reasonable remuneration for their work, why do people write? Depending on the genre you choose (genre meaning the category your writing fits into; for example, a memoir or novel), the reasons for writing vary. These may include:

A wish to share experience; for example, by writing a true-life story.
To entertain others with novels, plays, sketches and short stories.

To educate, warn or inform others through writing general non-fiction.

To raise public awareness; for example, by writing articles on subjects you feel strongly about.

To promote a good cause; for example, by writing and producing campaign literature.

To heal yourself through diary or memoir writing.

To share and preserve a person's history through biographical writing.

To express deep feelings and emotions through poetry.

Regardless of which genre you are writing in, you will find the creative process truly amazing as notions, thoughts, settings, characters and descriptions miraculously rise from your subconscious and materialize into words. I am still amazed by the creative process, even after thirty years of writing. It's as though someone else takes over and guides my hand, which in a way they do – that someone is my subconscious. But more on that later. Let's get started with that important first step and start writing.

First step

Many of the emails I receive from those seeking help and advice about writing ask: 'How do I begin?' The person has the desire to write, they have done any necessary research and their ideas have reached fruition, but they just can't seem to get started. The spirit is willing, but the flesh is weak. As writers, we've all been there. You can think of any number of reasons why you shouldn't start writing, from changing a light bulb to washing the car or clearing out the cellar. Everything seems more urgent than sitting down to write. This is largely due to being afraid of writing and failing. While your thoughts are safely in your head they are marvellous, original and like nothing else anyone has ever written before, but as you set them down on paper they become less wonderful. Maybe even insipid and uninspiring. Surely everyone else's writing is better than yours? Do you really have a story to tell? Who would want to read this? You lose faith in your ability to write and tear up your work, or press the delete key and start all over again, often with the same result. Sometimes, overwhelmed by the enormity of the task, we don't start at all and our masterpieces remain firmly in our heads. As Steven Wright, the American comic and writer, said: 'I'm writing a book. I've got the page numbers done.' All writers have experienced 'writer's block', as it's referred to. Don't worry; it can be unblocked.

This is what you do: choose a quiet place where you intend to write. It's a good idea to use the same place (and time) each day for your writing so that you fall into a writing routine. I'll explain more about that shortly. Now, pick up your pen or switch on your computer and, thinking of the story you want to write, start writing down the words that come into your head. Don't worry if what you have written doesn't make much sense, seems irrelevant or contains poor grammar; you'll sort all that out later when you rewrite. The main objective has been achieved – you are writing. Let the words flow however they care to, just as they come. Then give yourself a pat on the back – the creative writing process has begun.

If nothing comes into your head then try one of the following exercises to kick-start your subconscious into action:

- Think back to your earliest memory and describe the scene in a small paragraph (about six sentences). When you have finished that scene, add a 'what if'. What if I had done or said this instead of that? What if I had taken a different route? What if that person hadn't been there? Now write another small paragraph describing the outcome. This is obviously pure fantasy, so you are writing creatively, imaginatively and from your subconscious.
- Once you've finished your 'what if', turn your thoughts to the story you want to write and construct a small paragraph applying the same 'what if' principle. The scene you choose doesn't have to take place at the beginning of your book; just write whatever comes into your head. Well done, you are writing creatively.
- Describe an object you can see; for example, a table or an apple in the fruit bowl. Imagine the person who made that object or picked the apple and write a paragraph about him or her. Obviously you are unlikely to know anything about that person, so you are writing creatively. Once the words are flowing, turn your thoughts to your story and write a paragraph as above, applying this imaginative approach to your characters.
- Concentrating on one of your senses, describe what you can see, hear, smell, taste or touch. It can be just a short paragraph, and then, once you have written that, think of a scene in your story. What can your characters see, hear, smell, taste and touch? Well done, you are writing creatively.

I've used these techniques in my own writing in the past and also in writing groups. They do work, whatever genre you are working in. You may not need to use them, but if you are struggling to write that opening paragraph then try the above. Once you have started writing, keep going until the words stop and then finish for the day. You can check your work, but don't try to force any more words from your imagination. That rush of creativity is always limited and if you try and force it to go further you'll achieve little and may lose faith in what you have written. Three hours a day is my maximum for writing creatively, after which I may check over another document, answer emails, etc., but I do not attempt any more of that creative first draft. I imagine the process of creative writing as having a basket full of words and once that basket is empty I have to wait until the following morning for it to be replenished. Ernest Hemingway, writer and journalist, described it as a 'well' that refills overnight from the spring that feeds it. The creative process needs to be respected for its limitations, as much as for what it gives us.

Writing Routine

The creative process is usually helped by having a writing routine: a place and time set aside for you to write and with a little ritual leading up to the writing. If you approach your writing in the same way every day, very soon you'll find that by the time you sit down to write your subconscious will be fired up and ready to go. Your imagination will instantly start producing the words you need to write creatively. Like Pavlov's dogs, which were trained to expect food and therefore salivate whenever they heard a bell ring, you can train your creative juices to start flowing on your command by following your writing routine. The process is called classical conditioning and is triggered by the ritual of your writing routine.

I've had the same writing routine for the last fifteen years: I rise early (at approximately the same time each morning), put on my joggers and a comfortable top and creep downstairs so I don't disturb my family. I make a large mug of coffee and then go through to the front room where I collect my paper, pen and the text I've written the day before. I then go into the living room and quietly close the door. I sit in the same chair and, with my coffee within reach, I begin by reading what I've written the day before, editing as necessary. By the time I come to the end of the previous day's work, my new words are ready to flow. I still use pen and paper for the first draft. I write very quickly, often unaware of my surroundings as my pen dashes across the page. As the author Ray Bradbury said: 'My stories run up and bite me on the leg – I respond by writing down everything that goes on during the bite. When I finish, the idea lets go and runs off.'

I know exactly what this author means. When 'the idea has run away' and my basket of words is empty I type what I've written into my computer – first the revised draft from the day before, and then my new work. I print out the new pages ready for revising the following morning. This is my writing routine and it works for me. Your routine is likely to be different to mine, to suit your work and family commitments, and will also take into account when you are at your most creative. Some writers are early birds, like me; some are night owls, while a few lucky writers can turn on their creative juices at any time of the day or night. However, most writers (although not all) need silence and no interruptions while they are writing that first creative draft. I certainly do. I can't even have music playing softly in the background while I'm concentrating. Stephen King, the bestselling author, calls it 'the door closed'; that is to say his study door has to be closed against interruptions while he is writing creatively. You'll soon discover the situation and time that suits you best and, once you do, I recommend that you keep to your routine. It will act as a catalyst for your day's creative writing.

'What shall I use to write?'

… Some people ask. You can use whatever you like for that first draft, which only you will see: pen and paper, Dictaphone or you can type it straight into the computer. However, if you are intending to publish your work, at some point you will need to type it into a word-processing document (such as Microsoft Word) so that it can be sent electronically by email. I explain about publishing in the third section of this book. Whatever medium you use for your writing, make sure you have at least one copy of your work. If you are using only pen and paper then I suggest you photocopy your work each day. Once your work is on the computer, back it up by saving it on a 'memory stick', a CD or to a 'cloud' – where a third party stores your data on the internet. I can't emphasize enough how important it is to back up your work. You've invested a lot of time and energy in your story and paper copies can become lost or accidently thrown away, and computers do fail. I always have three copies of my work: the paper copy, on computer hard drive and on 'memory stick'.

Revising Your Work

It has been said that writing is 1 per cent inspiration and 99 per cent perspiration. Although this is a misquote – Thomas Edison, the inventor, actually said, 'Genius is 1 per cent inspiration and 99 per cent perspiration' – the words still demonstrate the point admirably. Writing, as with most other creative endeavours, requires a lot of hard work, and what you achieve will be the result of your labour rather than any sudden insight – although inspiration will be your guide. That first creative draft will have been an adventure, as your story unfolds and your characters reveal themselves through various, often dramatic, situations. You will have been on an adrenalin-fuelled rollercoaster of emotion as you wrote that first draft. Now you will need to spend time revising and rewriting your work until it is as good as you can make it. Unless, of course, your writing is for your eyes only; then all that matters is that you are happy with what you have written.

Most writers, however, want to share their work, and before you submit it to a literary agent or a publisher you will need to ensure your work is as clear of imperfections as possible. While an agent or publisher might overlook a few typing errors, he or she will not be impressed if your work is littered with irritating and basic grammatical errors, has a lack of or inappropriate use of punctuation or is poorly set out. Agents and publishers are far too busy with other writers' work to spend time trying to decipher your illiterate text, and so what might have been a bestseller may never see the light of day. As the writer Isaac B. Singer said: 'The waste-paper basket is the writer's best friend.' Or to bring this quote up to date, the delete key on your computer keyboard should be your best buddy. Like many writers, I probably throw away more words than I keep as I strive for perfection, finding a better word or phrase, restructuring a sentence, exchanging one idea for another or rewriting a paragraph, page, chapter or even the whole book.

Revising and rewriting are just as important as that first creative draft. While rewriting is hard work, it is also marvellously satisfying as you hone and polish your work to as near perfection as you can make it. Time spent on revising your work can make the difference between it being accepted for publication or rejected. You can revise and edit on your computer or on a paper copy. I do both, as I find some errors and omissions easier to spot with print on paper than on screen. I revise a book at least six times before I send it to my agent. When I write an article – where the length of the piece is preset and words are therefore at a premium – I often revise it a dozen times or more. I also read the article out loud, as hearing it gives a new and more objective viewpoint. I ask myself: have I said everything I need to say clearly and concisely? Are any words superfluous and can they therefore be removed? Does the article flow easily from one point to the next? As Nathaniel Hawthorne, the nineteenth-century American novelist and short story writer, said: 'Easy reading is damn hard writing.'

A revised page from this book

It has been said that writing is *one percent inspiration and ninety-nine percent perspiration*. Although ~~strictly speaking~~ this is a misquote, Thomas Edison, inventor, actually said *genius is one percent inspiration and ninety-nine percent perspiration*, his words demonstrates the point admirably. Writing, as with most creativity, is the result of a lot of hard work rather than any dramatic and sudden insight. Once you have written that first creative draft you will be spending a lot of time revising and rewriting your work, unless it is for your eyes only, for example your diary, then all that matters is that you are happy with what you have written.

However, most writers at some point want to share their work with others and go on to seek publication. I deal with publication in the second half of this book but before you are ready to send out your work you will need to rewrite, edit and revise your work until you are happy with it and it is as devoid of imperfections as you can make it. As the writer, Isaac B Singer said, 'The waste paper basket is the writer's best friend.' As you work on your story you will throw away more words than you will keep as you find a better word of phrase, delete or restructure a sentences, or let go of what once seemed a good idea and replace it with something better.

By the time you have finished rewriting and editing As well as checking your spelling, grammar, and punctuation ask yourself does the story flow or could it be tightened? Does it make sense to others who don't know me? Have I given

12

In addition to checking your spelling, grammar, punctuation and layout (more on that later), ask yourself: does your story flow, and will others reading your work for the first time understand it? Have you given sufficient background information or far too much? I agree with Elmore Leonard, novelist and screenwriter, who said: 'Leave out the parts that people skip.' It's very difficult to be objective about your own work; having invested so much time in it, you're too involved. So if you have a family member or a close friend whose opinion you value, I suggest you ask them to read your work before you submit it to an agent or publisher. A fresh perspective is often invaluable for spotting inconsistencies or omissions, as well as seeing silly spelling and grammar mistakes that you have missed. I'm not suggesting you change your story purely as a result of your reader's comments; only that you listen to what they say and give their opinions serious consideration. Don't take their criticism personally; it is not you they are criticizing, but your work. So often we are overprotective of our writing – seeing it as an extension of ourselves, as our 'baby' – and thereby we miss out on an opportunity to improve it.

Spelling, Punctuation and Grammar

I am not going to spend time writing a tome about spelling, punctuation and grammar. This book is not big enough for that and there are thousands of very good books on the subject already, as well as websites that give online advice and tutorials. In the UK, teaching grammar in schools went out of vogue for a whole generation as it was felt it stifled creativity. But, as with many trends in education, attitudes have come full circle and grammar is now being taught in schools again.

Don't worry if you missed out; you don't need to *know* that you are writing in prose, as long as you *are*, or that an independent clause must contain a subject and predicate, as long as it does. If you read extensively you will absorb good grammar and sentence structure through example. But if you feel your written English isn't up to the task of writing your story and you seriously want to write, then you will need to set about improving your core skills, as you would before undertaking any new task. All colleges of further education offer day and evening classes in English language, as do distance-learning courses (for example, the Open University). You don't have to wait until you've finished the course to begin writing; you can hone your skills while you are writing your story.

Reading

I can't emphasize enough the importance of reading, especially the genre in which you wish to write. Not only will reading improve your sentence structure, vocabulary, spelling and language skills, it will also show you what makes a good book – its structure, layout and pacing. If you find a word you don't know the meaning of while you're reading then look it up in a dictionary or online. I also suggest you make a note of any interesting or unusual words or phrases you come across to improve the richness of your vocabulary. I love words, so I have a small notepad in which I make a note of any new words or phrases I come across that appeal to me. I've had the same notebook for over twenty-five years and some of the early jottings include: 'diversely opposed', 'pragmatism', 'a sense of entitlement' and 'youthful remembrance'. I may use a variation of these one day, so I keep my little book as an *aide-mémoire*. Now there's a neat phrase. If you don't know the meaning of *aide-mémoire* then look it up.

Spellchecker

Now a word about computer 'spellcheckers'. Most computer software includes spelling and grammar checkers. Use them, but with caution. While they are usually good for picking up basic errors (silly spelling mistakes, typing errors, extra spaces, omissions of capital letters, etc.), they are far from foolproof and often make errors of judgement far worse than your own. Here are some examples taken from the first fifty pages of my book *Damaged*:

'One of the couples were first-time carers and Jodie should never have been placed with them.' The spellchecker, not recognizing that in this context the verb needs to be in the plural, not the singular, highlighted were as being incorrect and suggested was as the replacement.

'Look who's come to see you, Jodie!' The spellchecker suggested whose, which is an entirely different word. Who's is the shortened form of who is or who has, while whose is the possessive form of who.

'The sound of Jodie talking to herself floated down …' The spellchecker wanted to use her instead of the reflexive pronoun herself.

'She dropped to her knees and started thumping her face and head viciously.' The spellchecker wanted to replace face with the plural faces.

Here are some further examples from my book *Another Forgotten Child*:

'I was grateful my children were so understanding …' The spellchecker, unable to recognize the past continuous verb tense, wanted to replace so understanding with understood.

'"Come on, dry yourself," I encouraged.' The spellchecker, unable to see that yourself was being used as a reflexive pronoun, wanted to replace it with you.

You don't have to know the grammatical terms, just that what you have written sounds grammatically correct while the spell-checker's suggestion sounds wrong. English is a very rich language and one of the upshots of this is that the same word or phrase can be used differently or have a nuanced meaning depending on its context. Computers are clever, but not so clever (yet) as to be able to recognize these subtle variations in language, so it highlights your word or phrase as being incorrect and then suggests an alternative based on a literal interpretation. If you have doubts about the accuracy of your spellchecker's suggestion then err on the side of caution and don't accept a suggested replacement until you have checked your word or phrase on one of the many English grammar websites or in a grammar book.

Computer Skills

Just as you will need to develop a reasonably good standard of English to be able to write your book, so you will also need to be computer literate, unless you are going to ask someone else to type up your work or pay an agency to do it, which is going to be expensive – probably more expensive than buying a personal computer. Although touch typing is a useful skill to have, as it allows you to type quickly, it isn't essential, and many authors and business people get by with two-finger typing. I taught myself to touch type and I average about eighty words a minute, which is very useful for replying to the many emails I receive, as well as for writing my books. However, as long as your computer and typing skills are sufficient to allow you to produce a word-processing document (in a program such as Microsoft Word) and send it electronically, you don't have to be a computer geek. Colleges of further education offer day and evening classes in typing and computer skills – for every stage, from absolute beginner to advanced programming. There are also private tutors who will teach you computer skills in your own home, although they don't come cheap. Likewise, the company that sold you your computer may also offer a service whereby they set it up in your home, connect you to the internet and show you the basics.

I suggest you buy a printer to go with your computer. They are relatively inexpensive and as well as giving you the chance to see your work in print – which can give you a new perspective, as the printed word looks different from the screen version – most printers are also scanners and photocopiers.

Layout and Structure

The layout of your work is very important when you submit it to a literary agent or publisher, so you will need to follow their guidelines. These can be found on their website or in their entry in writers' handbooks such as the *Writers' and Artists' Yearbook*. However, while your work is under composition, you can use whatever layout or font suits you. I use the font Arial, in size 12, which is also a standard format for submission. To adjust the font and font size go to the drop-down menu on your toolbar in your word-processing document. The number refers to the size of the characters – the higher the number, the larger the font size. I always work in double-spaced lines, which allows me room to annotate my work on the printed sheet and write in changes. Most agents and publishers will require you to submit your work in double-spaced lines too, even though you will be sending it electronically – by email. Line spacing can also be changed in the drop-down menu on the toolbar in your word-processing document.

Use black print type (it will already be set as the default), not any other colour, and not bold, and remember to paginate your work (that is, insert page numbers). Pagination isn't usually a default setting on word-processing programs, so you will need to select it from the drop-down menu on your toolbar. Generally, the width of the left- and right-hand margins, as well as the depth of the headers and footers (the spaces at the top and bottom of the page), are preset and standard on your word-processing software, so you don't have to worry about them. The top and bottom spaces on a page are usually 1 inch and the side margins are 1¼ inches, which are acceptable to agents and publishers. Don't align the right-hand margin (which is also known as justifying the margin) as it will create false spaces between the words. The left-hand margin is justified by default, but leave the right-hand one 'ragged'; that is, free.

Sentences, paragraphs and chapters need to be kept to similar lengths for ease of reading. You probably won't have noticed this uniformity while you have been reading books, and that in itself is a good sign – it makes for a smooth and fluent read. There is obviously flexibility in the length of sentences, paragraphs and chapters, and while some genres (Mills & Boon romances and Quick Reads, for example) have more defined requirements, generally it is not a good idea to leap from a chapter of 5,000 words to a chapter of 15,000 words as the pacing will falter and may even be lost. If, while you are reading, you find yourself looking for the next chapter break then the chapter is very likely too long. You should find yourself suddenly at the end of a chapter, eager to turn the page for the start of the next and wanting to read on.

Likewise if you have to read a sentence a second or third time to make sense of it then the likelihood is that the sentence is too long – possibly with too many clauses – or it may have failed grammatically. A paragraph should contain only one main idea and the sentences within that paragraph should expand, develop and explain that idea. Take a look at a book you have recently enjoyed and you consider a good read, and then spend some time analysing its sentence, paragraph and chapter structure. I think you will see what I mean.

The first line of each new paragraph should be indented by one tab space (which will be preset on your word-processing package), and a reminder: a sentence starts with a capital letter and ends with a full stop. Do not use commas instead of full stops; they are different. Leave one character space between the end of a sentence and the start of the next. Chapter headings should be in bold, with a double-spaced line beneath, and before the start of the first sentence. Include a title page at the start of your work; an example of this is on page iii.

Editing Agencies

There are agencies that will edit, revise and proofread your work, either online or by working on a paper copy sent through the post. Their pricing structures vary, but they usually charge per hundred words, so if you have a full-length book of 80,000 words or more it can be very expensive. If you are considering using an editing agency, it may be worth sending a sample chapter to begin with. It will be much cheaper than having the whole book edited, and while the agency won't be able to comment on your plot development and characterization, they will be able to offer you advice on your style and general language skills. But be wary of any agency that claims or implies in its advertising that they have connections with publishers and that you will therefore stand a much better chance of being published if you use their services. They may have connections, but ultimately whether your work is published or not will depend on the appeal and standard of your work, rather than 'connections'.

Creative Writing Courses

Many organizations offer creative writing courses, which you can attend in person or through distance learning: local colleges of further education, universities, private colleges and agencies and personal tutors. You will also, of course, find many online. If you attend a course in person, you will have the advantage of meeting your tutor and other budding writers regularly, which can be very morale-boosting. If you opt for an online or distance-learning course, be selective. There are many to choose from, and standards as well as what they offer can vary a great deal. Good online and distance-learning courses will assign you a tutor who will set you assignments and give you constructive feedback, and whom you can email and speak to on the phone, and possibly meet in person. Some well-established distance-learning courses – for example, the Open University – also give you the opportunity to attend a residential summer school, while The Arvon Foundation offers regular residential writing courses at beautiful locations around the country, where you are tutored in small groups by a published writer in your chosen genre.

Writing Groups

Most towns have at least one local writing group. They usually meet weekly in an informal setting, such as a room over a pub, a corner of a café or a member's home. These groups are not usually tutor-led as writing courses are, but consist mainly of fledgling writers such as yourself, and offer the opportunity for members to read their work and receive feedback from the other members. Those attending are often unpublished authors, or have a little experience of being published or (increasingly) are self-published, which is worth remembering when you are considering their opinions on your work. Writing groups vary in their success. Some are well established and chaired effectively, and their members offer constructive criticism on work presented to the group, while others can be quite destructive, with opinions being egotistical and even vicious. If you feel uncomfortable in a group, or that the criticism offered on your work isn't helpful, then leave the group and find another one. There are plenty. Writing groups advertise on the internet, on notice boards in local libraries, colleges and community centres, and in local magazines and newspapers.

Online writing communities

These are website-based and offer members the chance to post and share their work with other members online. There are many of these groups – thousands – large and small, with some more established and sophisticated than others. A few are hosted by publishing companies who also run writing competitions and will consider the work of some of the members. These chosen few are usually selected by other members through a voting system of positive reviews of the piece of work posted. Some of those selected are also published.

Writing can be a very lonely experience, especially when you first start, and these online writing communities can be morale-boosting and supportive, as well as offering feedback on your work. As with any writing group, you should give your opinions on other members' works kindly, politely and considerately, and receive their opinions on your work dispassionately, professionally and objectively. Because of the anonymity the internet allows, reviews online can sometimes become very personal and even vindictive. As with a local writing group, if you feel uncomfortable about the way you are treated in one of these online writing communities, or that the criticism posted about your work isn't helpful, then leave by closing your account, and go elsewhere. Writing and sharing your work should be fun.

SECTION TWO:
WHAT TO WRITE?

When I receive an email asking for my advice on writing, the sender usually has a clear idea of what he or she wants to write and is looking for advice on how to begin, or is asking for some feedback on something they've already written, or wants advice on how to publish their work. However, some who email say they want to write but don't know what to write. If you are a budding author with the burning desire to write, but are not sure what to write, then I suggest you start with something small – for example, an article, poem, short story or diary entry – rather than a full-length book. Writing something relatively short means that you are likely to complete the piece in a reasonable length of time and will gain confidence from watching your work take shape and reach fruition. This book is not long enough to explain in detail how to write in all the different genres, so I will give you a taste of each, hopefully with enough information to whet your appetite and make you want to find out more.

Articles

I began my writing career by writing short articles, first for the school magazine, and then freelance for local newspapers and national magazines. At that time there were only paper publications (there was no internet), but now, in addition to paper publications, there are thousands of interest-led websites and online magazines, which offer a wealth of opportunity to publish articles. Article writing can be very satisfying. I still write articles now. It allows you to write on a subject you feel passionate about, or learn about a topic you previously knew little of from researching it for your article. Editors of printed publications usually pay for the articles they publish, online publications not so much, but for a fledgling author, to see his or her work published is often reward in itself. I say more about how to publish articles in section three of this book, so now let us look at how to write an article.

You have chosen the subject matter of your article, done your research and have all the material you need to hand, including any photographs or artwork, so you are ready to begin. Bear in mind your target audience – for example, are you writing for teenagers, gardeners, builders or parents? Knowing your audience is crucial, as the content of your article, its tone and style will vary to suit your intended reader. Writing for teenagers, for example, is clearly very different in subject matter and style to writing for parents, financiers or trainspotters.

Choose a snappy, attention-grabbing heading to start your article. If you are not sure of the length or are short of ideas, look at some of the articles in the publications you are going to write for. Under your main heading write your opening paragraph. This will be a brief summary – an overview – of your article. Here is an example:

It's good to talk to plants
Yes, it's true. Talking to plants is not only good for your plants, it is also good for you. Research students in California have shown that plants grow faster when they are read to for at least ten minutes a day than those in a control group. An expected bonus was that those reading to the plants were generally healthier than their counterparts too!

We have the eye-catching heading, and then the opening paragraph keeps the interest going with a flavour of what is to come. All paragraphs should be short and reasonably uniform in length, but long enough to make a point or develop an idea. Again, look at the articles in the publications you are aiming to write for and note the size and layout of the paragraphs and how they fit onto the page. Depending on the length of your article, you may need some sub-headings. These should alert the reader to the next point or sub-topic covered in the paragraph beneath it. For example, a sub-heading in our article about talking to plants might be: 'Do plants have favourite books?' Then, in the paragraph beneath, you'd discuss if the reading material used in the experiment affected the results; for example, did the plants prefer books on horticulture?

If your article needs artwork to illustrate certain points, insert it close to the relevant text. Photographs, drawings, charts, tables, etc., can be used to illustrate and support your points, but make sure you have permission to use these images. Copyright still applies on the internet, so don't just copy and paste a picture or chart from a website without obtaining the author's permission or you could be sued. Some articles may need an appendix and this should go at the end of your article. It is where you list your sources and any additional relevant reading material: by author, title, publisher and date of publication. As with all types of writing, read widely in the genre, thoroughly check spelling, grammar and punctuation before submitting, and keep copies of your work.

Poetry

Poetry is cross-cultural, universal and has a history going back to when the written word first evolved. Poetry is a succinct way of expressing emotion, and it need not rhyme. Poems can take many different forms – for example, narrative, ballads, sonnets, haikus and limericks. Some poems may be very short – haiku poetry, for example – or even one line: 'The most wasted of all days is one without laughter,' E. E. Cummings. Other poems, epic and ballad, for example, can be much longer. Homer's epic poems the *Iliad* and the *Odyssey* are over 200,000 words each – twice the length of an average book. But whatever its length, poetry is always concise, with no room for superfluous or redundant words. Poems work partly because of their structure and how they appear on the page.

Poems often use a variety of literary techniques, such as rhythm, imagery, alliteration and assonance to produce the emotion of the poem, and many people start writing poetry in response to a particularly emotional or difficult time in their lives. Writing poetry can be cathartic and often allows the writer to realize or release emotion, as the words spring from the subconscious onto the page. Poetry writing is now taught in many schools, so even quite young children can discover the joy of seeing their thoughts and feelings expressed in a poem.

A poem may capture a brief moment in time – look at many of the poems by T. S. Eliot and Ezra Pound, for example – or tell an entire story, as in *The Rime of the Ancient Mariner* by Samuel Taylor Coleridge, or *The Highwayman* by Alfred Noyes. The subject matter of your poem can be anything you choose. A successful poem will capture the feelings of the narrator at the time of the event, allowing the reader to experience similar emotions. If you are thinking of trying your hand at writing poetry then read a wide selection of poetry, classical and contemporary, including many different forms and styles. A poetry compendium, which will include works by many different poets, is a good place to start; for example, *The Oxford Book of English Verse*.

If you are a complete novice at poetry writing then I suggest you begin with a subject matter close to your heart. If you struggle for an idea then use the exercises on page 6. Let the words flow. Don't worry too much about line breaks or finding the best word to begin with. Just write your thoughts and feelings on your chosen topic. Once you have written the first draft of your poem, go through it and cross out all non-essential or superfluous words. Now put away your poem to work on another day. When you look at it afresh you will see plenty of room for improvement. Even though your poem may be short, you will find you need to work on it for days, weeks and months to improve it, changing a word here or tweaking a line there, or adjusting the rhythm and rhyme. Poetry is usually at its best when it is tight and concise: an image can say a thousand words. For example, consider the imagery used by Wordsworth in his famous poem *Daffodils*, or by D. H. Lawrence in *The Snake*. Good poems often appear deceptively simple, masking the many hours of hard work that go into their creation.

Because poetry often relies on a feeling – a moment of emotion – it is a good idea to carry a small notepad with you if you want to write poetry so that you can jot down any scene, situation, experience or feeling which has heightened meaning for you and might later make a poem, just as an artist draws a brief sketch of a scene to reproduce in greater detail on canvas later. These moments of heightened feeling or awareness often come without warning, darting into our consciousness and disappearing just as quickly. Easily lost, they can be likened to *déjà vu*. Making a note of your feelings at the time and what you saw, heard, smelt and tasted can serve as a reminder later – a handle, a prompt – from which you may be able to write a poem.

As well as serious and heartfelt poems, there are also many fun poems, such as limericks, ditties and children's poems. These often have a strong rhythm and rhyme, and a light-hearted subject matter. Different topics will suit different types of poetry, so experiment with a variety of forms and styles. There are no hard and fast rules when it comes to writing poetry, so enjoy. Everyone loves a silly ditty:

A circus performer named Brian
Once smiled as he rode on a lion.
They came back from the ride,
But with Brian inside,
And the smile on the face of the lion.

Short Stories

Short stories are a literary form in themselves; they are not just short books. They usually have one theme or main idea, a few characters, and tell a complete story. We've all written short stories as children at school, and very often the short story is a good place to start for the novice writer. Short stories can vary in length but are generally between 1,000 and 7,000 words – any longer and the story is usually referred to as a novella. A short story can be divided into sections or parts (if appropriate), by a change of scene, for example, but they don't usually have chapters.

If you are thinking of writing a short story then read widely from the many collections of short stories that are available in books, magazines, periodicals and some newspapers. Many authors who are famous for writing full-length novels also write short stories. It is a valuable exercise to read some of these and note how the author adapts his or her novel-writing style to accommodate the short story. Short stories often open abruptly – in the middle of a scene – and have a twist at the end. As with poetry writing, you can't afford to waste words in short stories.

A short story will often depict an extract from life – a snapshot – and leave the reader with an emotional response similar to that experienced after reading a poem. While characters in short stories need to be rounded to make them believable, description of the characters needs to be very concise, because of the limitation on words, and is usually best achieved through the character's actions and the plot. Conversations between characters will be necessarily limited. You can't, for example, have characters whiling away the time of day or chatting about the weather (unless it adds to the plot), as you might in a full-length novel or play. Dialogue usually accounts for about a third of the overall word count and must add to the plot or characterization.

As with any piece of writing, you will need to decide at the outset from which viewpoint you are going to narrate your story: first, second or third person. First and third person are the most popular viewpoints for fiction writing. First person is 'I' – that is, you are telling the story from your viewpoint: 'I woke to the sound of thunder crashing overhead.' Second person is 'you' – the narrator addresses a second person and adopts their perspective, telling the story from the addressee's point of view rather their own: 'You blush as you walk into the lecture late. The tutor pauses and all eyes turn towards you.' Third person is 'he', 'she' or 'it', and the narrator tells the story from an omniscient – all-seeing – perspective: 'Jeremy skipped down the garden path thinking he was the luckiest person alive.' Third person is a very useful perspective and also the most popular, as it allows the author to see all the action going on everywhere in the story, and also know what multiple characters are thinking and feeling as well as saying.

The setting and context of a short story need to be established quickly, and because of the limitation on words characters are not likely to move around much. The craft of short story writing lies in creating an intriguing plot – with conflict and tension – which rises to a dramatic climax (the height of the story) and has a believable resolution. The climax and resolution usually come close to the end of the story, and a clever short story will leave you deep in thought. Don't be put off if all this sounds a bit daunting; as with all other forms of writing, my advice is to read widely, start writing and then polish your story on your rewrites.

Diaries

This is not a diary of appointments but a record of the diarist's life. Anyone can write a diary and the form has been popular for hundreds of years. Many politicians and other famous and influential figures have published their diaries, allowing the public an insight into a world they would not otherwise see. One of the most famous early diarists was Samuel Pepys (1633–1703), who kept a diary for ten years during the seventeenth century, which documented such historic events as the great plague of 1665 and the great fire of London in 1666. Charles Darwin recorded his epic voyage of discovery in the 1830s in what has become known as his *Beagle Diary*. The famous diary of Anne Frank details the daily struggles of a fourteen-year-old Jewish girl while living in hiding from the Nazis during the Second World War.

Diarists should not be confused with authors who use the diary form to write a novel; for example, Daniel Defoe in *A Journal of the Plague Year* (1722), Sue Townsend in *The Secret Diary of Adrian Mole, Aged 13¾* (1982) or Helen Fielding in *Bridget Jones's Diary* (1997). These authors have used the diary as a literary device for writing a novel, so their work is fiction. Diarists record life as they see it and are therefore writing non-fiction.

Most people writing a diary do so first and foremost for themselves. However, it should be remembered that any words committed to paper (or computer) have the potential to be discovered and read by others, so if your diary is very revealing and truly for your eyes only, keep it secure. Writing a diary is not only a good way of recording your life and what's going on in the world around you; it can also be cathartic, releasing feelings and emotions that may be difficult or painful. Many writers, including myself, find writing cathartic. The process of delivering words onto paper (or a computer screen) seems to give them objectivity, allowing the writer space to explore and come to terms with difficult experiences and painful emotions. As the writer Graham Greene said: 'Writing is a form of therapy; sometimes I wonder how those who do not write escape the madness, melancholia, the panic and fear which is inherent in a human situation.' Diary writing is also known as journal writing and is sometimes used in therapy. Whatever your reason for writing a diary, here are a few tips to get you started:

- Choose a large diary or notebook to use as your diary because once you start writing you'll find you have plenty to say. You don't have to use a conventional diary; a large notebook which you divide up into days, weeks and months as you go works well.
- Make your diary attractive by decorating its cover with drawings, cut-out pictures and photographs, or by covering it in appealing wrapping paper. You could also illustrate your diary entries with sketches and photographs. Your diary should be an attractive and enticing place for you to go.
- Record significant daily events in chronological order, starting with early morning and continuing through your

day until night time. You don't have to detail every event, just what is significant and relevant to you. It's your diary, so you choose what you include.

- When describing events, include where appropriate what you saw, heard, tasted, smelt or touched. It will help you rekindle the scene when you read the entry in years to come.

- When describing emotions try to say what caused them. If you were sad, upset or deliriously happy then say why. Also try to be objective when you describe other people and situations. Our attitude and impression of others often changes over time and an objective portrayal will be more beneficial to you when you reread your diary in years to come.

Internet diaries and blogs

There is now a growing trend for ordinary people, as well as celebrities, to post their diaries or blogs on the internet, and some of those have become famous and been made into books. However, while you are reasonably safe confiding your inner-most thoughts and feelings to your personal diary, you need to think very carefully before you post anything on a website where thousands (even millions) could read it. Before you do, ask yourself if you would be happy if your boss, work colleagues, partner or family read it. And even more importantly, would they be happy with what you have written? The law of libel exists online – across all countries – just as it does with physical publications (i.e. printed). If you post something online that is defamatory about another person, company or product – even though it is your diary or blog and therefore only your opinion – you can be taken to court and sued. Writers have a responsibility for their words, wherever they are published.

Memoirs

Memoirs, also known as true-life stories or inspirational memoirs, are my speciality. It is within this genre that I am best known and have enjoyed much success. Inspirational memoirs have become so popular in recent years that they are now a genre in their own right, separate from – or a category of – biography. Whereas a biography usually objectively details a person's whole life and is often written in the third person, memoirs usually concentrate on a set period in a person's life and are written in the first person. My fostering memoirs, for example, tell the emotional and dramatic stories of the children I foster. Inspirational memoirs are very intimate and often depict the personal journey of the writer who has had to show great courage to overcome an experience or adversity. An inspirational memoir, therefore, requires emotional investment from the author and also the reader. Readers of my fostering memoirs often email me to say they laughed and cried openly while reading my books, as though they were in the room with me, feeling what I felt.

Just as diary writing can be cathartic, so too can writing your memoir. However, if you intend to publish and you refer to others in your book then again you will need to be mindful of the laws relating to libel. I say more of this later in the second part of this book on publishing your work. For now, let's get down to the business of writing your memoir. Your book will need to be approximately 85,000 words in length. Use the standard A4-sized paper, double-spaced lines, Arial font, 12 point. You will need to break down your story into chapters and give each one a title relevant to the action in that chapter. You will also need to decide on a working title for your book. Memoirs often have a brief introduction or preface to set the context of the book, and usually have an epilogue which allows the author to bring the reader up to date on recent events or those that happened after the end of the book. While 85,000-plus words may seem like a Herculean task, when approached in the context of your daily writing routine it is manageable. If you have already begun writing your memoir or you have written it, you may like to go over your work one more time, bearing in mind my advice. I believe the guidelines that follow contain the secret of writing a good inspirational memoir – the secret of my success.

- Write straight from your heart. Share your worries and anxieties with your reader, just as you share your jubilation.
- Take time to think back and remember. When and where did it all begin? Where were you? How old were you? Put yourself in that place while you write.
- Remember the settings. Describe them, and also anything significant or especially poignant in what you could see, hear, smell, taste or touch. Describe what was going through your mind.
- Be there and relive it, painful though this may be. Your strength lies in knowing your story inside out and better than anyone else.

It may be very upsetting, even traumatic, for you to go back and relive your past if you have suffered, so make sure you are ready to write your story. If you are not then postpone the project until you feel the time is right. There is no rush. I wrote my adopted daughter's story, *Will You Love Me?*, only after publishing sixteen other books, when she was a young adult. My eyes well and a lump rises to my throat whenever I write one of my fostering memoirs as I relive the scenes, even though it may be many years after the events. However, that is part of the success of my books, for as I relive what happened, so do my readers.

I always have an aim for my inspirational memoirs and so should you: the message you want to impart to your readers. It may be one of courage, faith, hope, a determination to succeed at something or simply to survive an ordeal. Keep your aim in mind as you write, and remember: when you write your true-life story you have an emotional contract with your reader that you don't have when writing fiction. You owe your reader honesty and integrity, and in return you will have your reader's unfailing empathy and support. I have been completely over-whelmed by the thousands of emails I've received from my readers and their lovely comments about my fostering and writing.

Write scenes into your book; don't just present a monologue as you might in a diary. Although the memoir is true it doesn't have to be a diatribe of abuse and suffering. I write my memoirs as I would a gripping novel: building scenes, creating tension and using cliff-hangers at the end of chapters to keep the reader's interest. Dialogue – that is, what people say to each other –

is important in inspirational memoirs as it will help you develop scenes and characterization, as well as advance the plot and break up the text. There is more advice on writing dialogue on page 61. There will be highs and lows in your story, so use them to keep the reader on a roller-coaster of emotion. There may be some very sad scenes, some horrendous incidents, and also light-hearted or even funny incidents. If there is constant, unrelenting degradation and abuse the reader will soon become desensitized and lose empathy and therefore interest.

Make your book episodic, by which I mean describe in detail events that are of interest or highly poignant to your story and leave out the mundane, unless it is an intrinsic part of building the scene. You can telescope many years of real time into a couple of lines or develop fifteen minutes into a whole chapter (or more) if it merits it. For example, look at the way I receive the news of Tayo's father in *Hidden*, or when I am awaiting the arrival of Reece in *Mummy Told Me Not to Tell*, or the days before Jade is about to have her baby taken into care in *Please Don't Take My Baby*. To help hone your skills, read plenty of inspirational memoirs, consider how the author uses the above techniques and then write with passion. As William Wordsworth said: 'Fill your paper with the breathings of your heart.' This is a beautiful quotation and one I've kept close to me for many years.

Biography

I receive emails from budding authors who are setting out to write a biography – either their own (autobiography) or that of someone else, possibly a family member or a close friend. Sometimes these biographies are intended for family use only, as a legacy to pass down to future generations. However, if the subject of the biography has achieved something outstanding or has led a very unusual or interesting life that may be of interest to others, then publication is sought (see the third section of this book for advice about publishing).

As mentioned previously, a biography differs slightly from a memoir. It is likely to be more objective and written in the third person (unless it is an autobiography, which will be written in the first person), and will detail the person's life chronologically. If you are writing a biography about someone other than yourself and that person is still living, explain your project to that person and ask their permission to write their biography. If the person is dead then discuss your project with the person's next of kin or close family and try to obtain their permission. Not only will a publisher expect this, but it is also polite, and family members will be a valuable source of information. Research is the cornerstone of a good biography. Here are some guidelines:

- Look for anything by or about the person: in books, newspapers, magazines, diaries, letters, videos or on the internet.
- Interview the person you are writing about (if possible). Interview their family, friends and work colleagues; in fact, anyone who knew the person. A face-to-face interview is ideal, but interviews can also be conducted over the phone or by email.
- Visit places where the person lived or places that were significant to the person, and imagine them there. 'Walk in their shoes' so you can see the area from their viewpoint; it will give you a greater understanding of your subject matter. If it is impractical to visit these places, research them online and/or in books. The better informed you are about the subject matter, the more interesting your biography will be.
- Take photographs, include pictures and newspaper and magazine cuttings, and photocopy relevant certificates. Keep originals in a safe place and only use photocopies for your book.
- While you are researching the biography, think about the person's personality. What were their interests? What influenced and inspired them? What made them laugh or cry? Include anecdotes. Was the person generally in good health? Did they have a robust constitution? Were they generally optimistic or of a pessimistic disposition? The more detail you include about the person, the more he or she will come alive in your biography.
- A good biography not only tells the story of the person's life, but also shows the time and society in which that

person lived. Research what was happening socially, economically and politically at the time the person lived. How did this impact on the person?

- Check and validate all your facts and sources. Just because something is written online doesn't mean it is fact.

If you are writing your own life story (autobiography) then your research should be much easier, as you are likely to be already in possession of much of the above information. Research what you don't know and interview others. Hearing what others have to say about you (a teacher, for example) will allow you to give a fuller and more objective picture of yourself.

Once you have the information you need for the biography, draw up a timeline – a chronology of events – showing the date and what happened. This is to help you write your book so that you can include events in the correct order. You can also include a short one-page timeline at the start or end of your book if you wish. Now decide on a working title and think about how the book will be broken into chapters. Chapters can be adjusted as you work, but it is useful to have a framework for the biography before you start.

Using the standard double-spaced lines on A4 paper, begin. Although your biography will be in chronological order, start with something interesting and not just the date on which the person was born. Show scenes that give insight into the person's personality, anecdotes that shaped them and made them the person they became. What life events impacted most on their decision making? What effect did they have on others? Using your research, imagine yourself in the person's shoes. Although a biography is factual, you can conjecture by prefacing your comments with: 'although we can't be certain, it is likely that ...' or 'we can imagine the impact this news had on ...' or 'quite possibly this was the reason for his decision to ...'

End your biography on a positive note, with a résumé of the person's achievements and the latest information you have on them; for example: 'Alex will shortly be fulfilling his dream of retiring to the Caribbean where he will continue his good work.' If the person is dead, end the biography with the circumstances and date of their death and the legacy he or she left behind. A reflective quote from someone who was close to the person works well. As with any piece of writing, if you've quoted from another person's work then you must acknowledge it in the appendices at the end of your book. Don't forget to paginate your work and back it up with copies, and of course read other biographies.

Non-Fiction

Non-fiction is a general category of writing that covers all factual books. The subject matter of these books is vast and includes history, science, engineering, gardening, psychology, travel, manuals, self-help guides, textbooks, biographies and memoirs. If you are thinking of writing a non-fiction book, you will probably already know your subject matter well; if not, research thoroughly in books, newspapers and magazines and on the internet. Not only will you be gathering information, but you will also be checking to make sure you are bringing something new to the subject and not just repeating work that has already been published. Popular non-fiction subjects such as gardening, cookery, slimming, Jane Austen or how to get rich quick have been written about extensively. If you are thinking of writing on a popular subject, find a new angle with which to approach the subject matter or add something fresh and exciting to what has already been written.

Once you have all the information you need, including relevant photographs, tables, diagrams, etc., think how you are going to divide up your work – into chapters, or sections and sub-sections? Consider what information you are going to include in each section or chapter, bearing in mind your target audience. A do-it-yourself (DIY) book for beginners, for example, is going to be very different in style and content to one aimed at experienced DIY enthusiasts, just as a mathematics textbook for a class of twelve-year-olds will be pitched very differently to one intended for university students. Plan your book thoroughly before you start. Each chapter, section or subsection can be adjusted as you work, but before you begin you want a clear plan of what is going where so that the information is presented logically, without repetitions or omissions.

Decide on a working title and, using the standard A4 format and Arial font, 12 point, with double-spaced lines, begin. Work methodically using your plan as a guide, concentrating on a section or chapter at a time. The great advantage of working on a computer with word-processing software is that you can move a sentence, a paragraph or even a whole chapter if you find it is better suited to a different part of your book. As in all other writing, if you quote or use information or original ideas from another author's work (which is common in non-fiction, where authors present their ideas in the context of previous work), then you need to acknowledge your source. Asterisk the words or lines on the page where they appear and cross-reference them to the bibliography at the end of your book. All work quoted should show the author and title of the piece, the publisher and date of publication. Don't ever be tempted to use another author's work without acknowledging it. Not only can you be sued for plagiarism, but your reputation as a writer will be tarnished.

Non-fiction books generally have a contents page at the beginning and an index at the end. You will need to adjust the page numbers on your contents page once you've finished revising your work as the page numbers will change while you work on the document. For this reason, too, indexing should be left to the very end if you are self-publishing or left to the publishers to organize once the book has been typeset. When you have the first draft of your book, revise and edit it as necessary. Check with your plan that you have covered all the material you intended. Ask yourself if you have achieved the aim of your work, and if it is appropriate for your target audience. If you have a friend or family member whose opinion you trust then ask him or her to read your book, and then consider their feedback. That you have written a non-fiction book suggests you want to impart your knowledge to others, and information on publishing non-fiction books is in the second section of this book.

Novels

A novel is a work of fiction; that is, it is made up. Novelists, especially those writing their first novel, often base their story on an incident, situation or experience they are familiar with, and their characters are often people they know or have known in the past. While this is acceptable – many storylines originate from an incident or chance encounter that sparks the author's imagination, and some people do make great caricatures – be sure the people in your story are not so thinly veiled that they can be identified. You can be taken to court for defamation, even though you've changed the characters' names, if they can be identified. Don't ever be tempted to wreak revenge on someone you feel has slighted you or done you wrong by writing them into a novel – you will be discovered for sure.

There are many different categories (also known as genres) of novel, and you will need to decide at the outset what type of novel you want to write. Will it be horror, crime, mystery, romance, western, historical, science fiction, fantasy, thriller or erotica, for example? There is also 'general fiction', sometimes known as 'popular', 'commercial' or 'mass-market fiction', which appeals to a wide audience, and 'literary fiction', which is generally considered to be more 'serious' in content than 'popular fiction', and some would say has more literary merit. Each category or genre of novel has its own style of storytelling, although they all share some common principles.

Read widely in your chosen genre, analyse what works well and why some novels are more successful than others. This book is not big enough to detail all you need to know about writing in each category of novel, so I'm concentrating on the guidelines that apply to all.

First, let's look at the ingredients necessary to make a good novel:

- A sound plot leading to a dramatic climax, followed by a satisfactory resolution.
- Suspense, tension and emotional conflict.
- Whole, rounded characters.
- Empathy with the main protagonist (character).
- Believable scenes and settings.
- Realistic dialogue.

The above apply to all categories of novel, as do the following criteria for achieving a successful novel.

Planning your novel

Different authors approach writing novels in different ways. Some authors meticulously plan their books right down to the last detail before they start, while others have only the briefest outline – either jotted down or in their head. The majority (myself included) plan to some extent and then let the characters take over and shape the action. There is no right or wrong way to plan a novel, providing you do have a plan. If you are a novice writer, I suggest you write down your plan, even if it's just a few lines, rather than simply having the idea, which could be forgotten. As well as helping you to remember your story, the plan will also allow you to view your story objectively and check you haven't missed anything out. The plan should include a brief outline of your plot, pen sketches of the main characters and how they fit into the plot, and details of the setting – that is, the time and place in which your novel is set.

I also suggest you have a 'plan of action', which is the time frame in which you intend to write your novel. Authors who have a contract with a publishing house to write a book will have a deadline written into their contract, by which date they will have to finish the book and submit it to the publishers. If you don't have a publisher (and therefore a deadline), I suggest you set yourself a deadline and try to keep to it. If writing your novel becomes too protracted, you will lose the impetus of your storyline, lose enthusiasm, and eventually consign your partially written book to a bottom draw as a project for a rainy day. As with all long pieces of writing, it is advisable to write a little each day, which should be achievable as part of your writing routine. This will keep the momentum going and your goal of finishing in sight. Even if you just write one page a day, a year later you will have written 365 pages, which is the length of the average novel.

The plot

Stripped down to the very basics, all plots essentially comprise a central protagonist who overcomes a series of crises and conflicts, which are eventually resolved. Clearly the author fleshes out the story around the plot, creating suspense, heightening tension and allowing the reader enough information at any time to keep them interested without giving away the ending of the story. The opening of a novel is the start of your plot and must be sufficiently intriguing to grab the reader's attention. The majority of the book-buying public base their decision on whether to buy a novel from looking at the cover and then reading the blurb on the back and the first page. A publisher or literary agent is also likely to decide if they want to read your entire book from the opening page.

The first chapter of your novel will start the plot rolling, set the scene and introduce one or two characters. Don't go into too much background detail at the start of your book; you can fill in the history as the plot progresses. By the end of the first chapter the reader should have a good understanding of the nature of the drama that is to come; for example, in a romance novel the reader is likely to know that the heroine has been thwarted in love and is now in search of a soul mate. In a crime novel the nasty deed around which the plot revolves is likely to take place, and in science fiction the alien invasion is on its way. These are just examples, but whatever your plot, it should be rooted in the first chapter.

Following chapters will develop and escalate the plot, in which the central protagonist will be presented with a number of challenges, which, despite his or her best efforts, seem impossible to overcome. The tension builds towards the climax of the story, when the tide of misfortune and frustration dramatically turns. The hero or heroine's fortune changes, the plot is fully revealed and the resolution that follows is believable and satisfactory. As always, read widely in your chosen genre and note how the plots rise to a dramatic climax. No amount of tutoring compares to observing a master at work, and reading will help you to hone your plot-making skills. It is a good idea to end each chapter with a little cliff-hanger in your plot, so that the reader is eager to turn to the next page and read on.

Characterization

Before you begin your book you need to know your characters and what they are capable of. Characters are made believable by acting 'in character'; that is, doing what they are capable of. A character who acts 'out of character' will quickly lose not only their credibility, but the credibility of the author too. For example, you can have a psychopath strangling a puppy, but you couldn't have an elderly lady doing it (unless, of course, she was a psychopath). Don't spend too long describing the characters in the narrative voice – that is, you telling the reader about the character – a sentence or two is sufficient. Show your characters' personalities through their actions, the plot, how they interact with each other, and what other characters say about them. In real life, a person doesn't arrive with a résumé of their character written on their forehead; we learn about them as we get to know them, and so it should be in a novel.

The reader needs to feel empathy with the main protagonist (character) so they care about what happens to them, although they don't have to identify with them. Characters, even the 'goodies', have weaknesses and flaws as well as positive attributes, just as people in real life do. All characters in your book should have a role, even if it is just as the 'fall guy'; otherwise don't include them. Main characters will have more line space than minor characters, but all characters need to relate to the main protagonist either directly or indirectly. Children act differently to adults and men differently to women, so their responses to situations need to reflect this.

Setting and scenes

Setting the scene is important as it acts as a backdrop for your plot and characterization. You don't always have to describe the setting in the narrative voice (that is, tell your reader); you can have your characters commenting on their surroundings. Characters become more real and believable, and plots more plausible and riveting, if they are set firmly in a place and time. The reader will be able to imagine themselves there in the drama, appreciate how the characters are feeling and live through the trials and tribulations of the plot with them. Combining action with scene setting is a great device for keeping the action going: 'The rain soaked into her coat as she hurried down the street towards the house that was once her home.' The scene is set and we feel the atmosphere of the action. Or: 'The temperature in the room dropped as the door slowly creaked open and Jacob rose to his feet.'

'Show, don't tell' is a well-used and faithful maxim for writers, meaning that the author should build a scene to show the action, rather than simply telling the reader what happened. 'Showing' rather than 'telling' creates immediacy, encouraging the reader to feel they are there, participating in the action, rather than viewing it from a distance. As a writer, you can't make a scene out of everything you want to include in your book – no book is long enough – so you have to choose what information and action you develop into a scene and what you simply tell your reader. If a reader has to know that a teenager has a birthday, for example, it can be dealt with in a single line: 'Max was seventeen in July.' Or it could be developed into a scene if Max throws a party while his parents are out, which gets so out of hand that the police have to be called. The general rule is that a scene should be created when information or action is intrinsic to the plot, required to build tension, or essential to characterization. The narrative voice is used when the information is of less importance, but still needs to be known by the reader.

Dialogue

Dialogue is the spoken word; it is what characters say to each other. The words spoken are usually enclosed in speech marks, also known as inverted commas or quotation marks, either single – '…' – or double – "…" Each new speech by a character should be indented as a new paragraph. To demonstrate the point, here is a short extract from my book *Hidden*:

'Yes, they will,' I said. 'So you must be looking for a home for him. Has this young man got a name?'

'The duty officer doesn't know it.'

'So where is the child now?'

'I don't know.'

I raised my eyebrows. I was used to things often being rushed and confused in the world of fostering, but even I was surprised by the lack of information.

Dialogue needs to be in keeping with the person's character, and what they say should advance the plot, help create atmosphere or develop a character. There is no place in a novel for idle chatter, unless it is a necessary part of the plot, scene or characterization. Dialogue needs to be easily understood by most readers or they will become frustrated at having to reread lines, so use with caution dialect, snippets from a language you are not writing in, slang and colloquialisms.

Not only does dialogue advance the plot, develop scenes and characterization, but (because it requires a new paragraph for each new speech) it also visually breaks up the narrative, giving the reader respite from paragraphs of tightly printed text. Dialogue usually accounts for a third to a half of a novel and should be evenly distributed throughout, with the narrative voice flowing seamlessly into the dialogue and out again when the character finishes talking.

Dialogue, both in content and style, should be realistic in the context of the scene and in keeping with the character speaking. However, dialogue in a novel is not the same as dialogue in real life. Conversations in novels have to be contracted and succinct, imparting what the reader needs to know and leaving out all the 'ums', 'ers', hesitations and repetitions that litter normal speech. Men and women speak differently in real life, as do different ages and those coming from different backgrounds, and so they should in your novel. A mistake made by many writing their first novel is to have all the characters talking in the same manner. Different characters will speak differently just as they will look different and act and dress differently. A gentleman in his late seventies is unlikely to say 'that's cool' or ask for a 'high five' from a colleague, whereas a teenager or young person might. While reading your favourite novels, look at the dialogue, observe how it works and then write your own. As with any skill, practice makes perfect.

The ending

The ending of a novel is as important as its beginning and should gently draw the reader out of the story just as the opening drew the reader in. That is not to say the ending needs to be 'drawn out' by making it unnecessarily protracted, but you need to take time to consider how to close your novel. Endings need to be satisfactory and do justice to the time (and money) the reader has invested in reading your book. For example, a ghost story that ends 'I woke up with a start. It had all been a dream' is not acceptable; it is a 'cop-out', as are endings that are left to the reader's imagination, or are unrealistic or too abrupt. Don't introduce any last-minute surprises and expect the reader to accept them. Any twist or revelation at the end needs to have been previously (albeit unobtrusively) cemented firmly in the plot – the clue is there, should the reader see it. The reader ought to be led out of the story feeling satisfied, entertained and eager to read your next book. Write your ending as you complete the first draft of your novel and then revise it when you rewrite. We have all read novels with poor endings. A perfectly good story can be undermined by a less than satisfactory conclusion. The words at the end of your story are the last your reader will see, so do your book justice by making them as near perfect as you can.

Plays

Writing a play, whether it is for television, radio, stage or film, is a craft in itself. Although they all require a script, these different media require different methods of presentation. A play written for the stage, for example, will be different in content and presentation to a play written for the big screen. There will be limitations in the elaborateness of the plot, stage setting and cast of characters. A play for radio, where the playwright relies on dialogue and sound effects, will require a different script to one written for the stage, television or big screen. Shortly I will set out some general guidelines that apply to all playwriting, but first a few words of advice.

As with all types of writing, if you are a novice it is advisable to start small: a short play with a few characters and a simple setting, one that could possibly be staged at home or in a village hall. An unknown playwright is not likely to attract the attention of a Hollywood film producer, but your friends, family and a small local audience may well be interested. Start small and grow. Get involved in your local amateur dramatics society – most towns have one. You will be able to gain an insight into the practicalities of staging a play as well as having fun. Watch and listen to plays – on radio, television, theatre and the big screen. Enjoy them as entertainment, but also consider how they work.

Some successful plays have had their scripts published. I suggest you read a selection and consider them in relation to various productions of the play you have seen. It is worth seeing more than one production of a play so that you can compare and contrast the different interpretations. Before you start writing your play, consider the cost of staging it. It is more likely to be taken on by a director of television, radio, stage or screen if it is economical to produce. Some very successful plays and films were made on very small budgets.

Plot

Just as a novel has a plot, so too does a play. It is the plot, or storyline, that keeps the audience's attention. It will be episodic, with highs and lows, as your central protagonist overcomes various obstacles until the play reaches its climax and all is revealed in the resolution. Write the outline of your plot (about a page in length) before you begin writing your actual script. Also write an outline of the action that is to take place in each scene, so you have a guideline and can pace the plot. Consider the length of your play, decide on the characters, the settings (or locations, if it is a play for the screen) and your target audience. When you are considering your plot, remember to take into account your medium – theatre, radio, television or film – as there will be different practical requirements. The opening of your play will start the plot and set the scene, introduce a few characters and immediately draw the audience into the action through intrigue, leaving them curious to see what happens next. Your play will also need a satisfactory ending so that the audience departs with that glow from being thoroughly entertained, even if your play or film has dealt with a sad or serious subject matter.

Cast

The cast comprises the characters in your play and will be chosen by you as you plan your plot. Decide on their gender, age, background and ethnicity, what they look like and how they dress. Even if you are writing a play for radio where the characters can't be seen, you still need a clear picture in your mind of your characters so that they are fully developed and come 'alive'. Think about how they speak and behave, and carefully consider the number of characters your play requires; the more you have, the more actors you will need who will have to be paid and the more expensive your play will be to perform or film.

Develop the characterization as your plot unfolds. Your audience will need to be able to empathize with the main protagonist. Screenplays and plays for the stage give the writer the advantage of being able to develop their characters through appearance as well as dialogue. Use this to its full advantage – think about how a character dresses, their mannerisms and other visual nuances, all of which contribute to their characterization. Radio clearly relies on the auditory sense alone, so in addition to carefully crafted dialogue, capitalize on intonation, exclamations, timed pauses, sound effects and what the characters say about each other. Characters need to be believable and to behave consistently in plays, just as they do in all other genres of writing. A short description – a couple of lines – about each character can be included beside their name on the cast sheet. For example:

DAVE SMITH: Early forties, overweight, grey hair, missing
   right arm.

If an actor is going to play more than one part then that should
be recorded on the cast sheet too.

Settings and locations

Intrinsic to the plot will be the settings for your play or the locations for your film. The settings or locations provide the backdrop
for your plot and characterization. Consider the historical time
and geographical location of your play or film – that is, where
and when it is set. This will clearly need to be reflected in the
scenery. Make the setting interesting; it doesn't have to be lavish,
just intriguing and relevant to your plot and characters. Think
carefully about the number of changes in setting or location. Too
many changes or very elaborate settings could make the play or
film impossible to produce. Some very successful plays and films
have relied on only one or two sets. Your settings or locations will
also vary depending on the type of play you are writing. A radio
play, for example, will require very different props – mainly
sound effects – compared to television, stage or film productions,
which will be largely visual. Details of sets or locations are
included in the script at the start of each scene. For example:

INT. DINING ROOM OF A MODERN FAMILY HOME. THE
FAMILY ARE IN THE MIDDLE OF THEIR EVENING MEAL.

'INT' is always used to denote interior settings and 'EXT'
outside.

Directions

Stage directions, as they are known, are written into the script. They advise the production team and cast of the characters' actions and movements. As a playwright you will need to think carefully about the logistics of how your characters come onto and leave the stage or film set, and how they move around while on the set. Some of the actors' movements – gesticulations, for example – can be left to their own interpretation of the role, but generally you will need to show through the directions where they should be while performing.

Consider the limitations of the type of play you are writing. A radio play or a film, money permitting, can have a cast of thousands gathered in crowd scenes, for example, but a theatre production cannot. Likewise, to have a character showering is quite easy to produce in a radio play through sound effects, but it is far more complex to achieve onstage where running water is required. If your character must have a shower, then a solution would be to have him shower offstage, using a recorded sound effect of someone showering, and then appear onstage with a towel wrapped around him and with damp hair. Directions should be written in the present tense and should be concise, clear and easy to follow. For example:

DEBBIE gives a cry and runs to ALAN.

Dialogue

Dialogue is the words spoken by the characters in your play and it will form the basis of your plot – your storyline relies on it for its success. Dialogue will form the majority of your script, so it is what makes or breaks a play. Characters need to speak in character at all times to make them credible, and their dialogue must appear realistic, though not exactly as people speak in real life. Dialogue on stage or in a film needs to be direct and succinct, leaving out all the 'ums', 'ers', hesitations and repetitions that are in normal conversations. Dialogue needs to be easily understood by the audience, so avoid strong dialects and obscure quotes, slang or colloquialisms. Dialogue will advance the plot, build tension and develop characterization. Dialogue should convey information, but subtly, so it doesn't appear contrived. If you need to tell the audience something very important that is crucial to their understanding of the play then repeat the information, but in a different way, possibly by having another character rephrase or comment on it. For example:

DAVID: You do understand why it was impossible for me to keep seeing Angie after she lied about her age?
LISA: Absolutely. I can't believe she told you she was eighteen. She was fifteen then and technically a minor.

All dialogue, including any asides (where the actor speaks directly to the audience) and voiced thoughts, must be written into your script. Dialogue can be emotional, but not melodramatic, and should never state the obvious. For example:

KEVIN: Here comes Shane [when he has just walked onstage].

Far more natural to put:

KEVIN: Hi, Shane. Good to see you.

Dialogue in a play or film goes hand in hand with the directions so that the actors know what they are doing while they speak their lines. Characters address each other, but the audience, including those at the very back, obviously need to be able to hear. This is why traditionally stage actors are told not to turn their backs on their audience – their voices are projected to the back of the stage instead of to the audience, as are their facial expressions (an important form of non-verbal communication), resulting in both being lost. Include wit and humour in your dialogue. Audiences need to laugh sometimes, even if the play is sad. Be careful, though – tragedy can become bathetic, resulting in loss of empathy and credibility for you and your work, if humour or emotion is used inappropriately. Read your dialogue out loud; the spoken word often sounds very different from the written word. Time the play, and if your speeches are too long, cut and tighten as necessary. You can't afford to waste words in a play or film, or the audience will become bored and lose inter-est. Study the dialogue in other good scripts, but don't plagiarize.

The script

At some point you will need to type your script into the correct format. Scripts for theatre, radio, television and film vary slightly, but here are the basics common to all. Use A4 paper, Arial font in point size 12, with 1-inch margins at the top, bottom and each side, unless you're binding your script, in which case leave a left-hand margin of approximately 1½ inches. Use single-spaced lines with an additional blank line between a character's dialogue and the stage directions. Paginate the script, but not the title, cast or setting page. If your play has more than one act, then number the acts and scenes consecutively throughout the script. You may want to invest in some computer software for writing plays. This presets the layout of the script to guide you. It is relatively inexpensive and can save a lot of time.

Begin your script with the title page. This will state the title of your play, your name and contact details or those of the literary agent representing you. Next will be the cast page where you list all your characters. Capitalize the names of the characters and then beside each name give their age, gender and anything else that is essential to casting. Here is a short example:

CAST OF CHARACTERS
MARY, thirty-something mother of two boys
JACK, her fifty-year-old husband
SIMON, mid-twenties, the milkman

Do not write lengthy descriptions about the characters, as the play will develop characterization.

Next is the setting page, which contains a brief paragraph detailing the setting for the play and the time in which it is set. For example:

SETTING

*A Victorian townhouse in an upmarket London street. A log fire
burns brightly in the magnificent marble fireplace. Antique vases
and furniture litter the room and copies of* Country Living
magazine are on the onyx coffee table.

TIME

Winter. The present. Evening on the last day of January.

Some playwrights include a synopsis of the scenes on the
setting page, but it is not obligatory. Here is an example:

SYNOPSIS OF SCENES

ACT I
Scene 1: Sitting Room. Evening of 31 January.
Scene 2: Main Bedroom. That night.
Scene 3: Breakfast Room. The following morning.
Scene 4: Sitting Room. The following evening.

ACT II
Scene 1: Main Bedroom. Night. A week later.
Scene 2: Breakfast Room. The following morning.

Next is the actual body of the script where the action takes
place. For example:

ACT I, SCENE 1
*MARY and MARK are relaxing in their living room over after-
dinner coffee when the milkman bursts in.*

MARK: Who let you in?

MILKMAN: I don't need letting in. I have a front-door key.

MARK: [*Standing*] Since when does the milkman have a front-door key?

MARY: Since I gave him a key.

Try out your play on family and friends or your local amateur dramatics society, if you are a member. Consider their feedback carefully and rewrite as you see fit. Suggestions for submitting plays are in the second section of this book. Most importantly of all, enjoy. Writing plays and performing them should be great fun.

Children's Books

You will need to decide on the age range of children you want to write for. A pre-school picture book designed for very young children, for example, is quite different from an adventure story for eight-year-olds or teen fiction. Whatever age group of children you write for, read widely in that age range, and also look at the children's books stocked in nurseries, schools, libraries and the children's section of bookshops. Although writing for different ages of children varies in content, form and style, here are some general guidelines that can be applied to all:

- Don't lecture, patronize or talk down to children. Children will notice and won't warm to you or your story. Try to think back to when you were a child and write with that fresh inquisitiveness and vibrancy that comes naturally to children.
- Create characters who are individuals and interesting, and who will inspire the child. The main character, as in adult fiction, will overcome a number of obstacles during your story until all turns out well in the end. Your story must have a happy or hopeful ending where the good guys win and the bad guys lose.

- Magic and wizardry can happen in your story, but you will need to convince your audience that it is true. The best way to do that is to believe in it yourself.
- Your storyline needs to be fast paced. The text needs to be tight, so delete any unnecessary words or sentences. Include only brief descriptions in the narrative voice as the plot moves forward.
- Make sure your book has a good text-to-picture balance appropriate for the age group you are writing for. A picture book designed for pre-school children, for example, will contain one or two lines of large-print text per page and a large picture which illustrates the text.
- Make sure your book has a good dialogue-to-narrative balance appropriate for your reader's age group. Dialogue brings characters to life as well as advancing the plot.
- Use the same tense and narrative viewpoint throughout your book. If you start in the first person and the present tense, stay in it. Even teenagers can find changes of tense and perspective confusing when reading a story.

Read your story out loud. Read it to friends, family and children in the age group for whom it is intended. If the book is for older children, give them a copy of your book to read. Children are uninhibited and make good critics.

If you are unable to create the artwork for your book, you can either link up with an illustrator or include a brief description of the picture you imagine on the relevant page when you submit your work to a publisher or literary agent. Large publishing houses have their own in-house illustrators or will use a freelance illustrator if they publish your work.

Ghostwriting

Writing a book for someone else is called ghostwriting. There are professional ghostwriters who will write your book for you – usually your memoir or biography – for a fee or a percentage of the royalties. People use ghostwriters if they feel they have a good story to tell but are not up to writing it themselves. While I wouldn't dream of advising a professional ghostwriter how to write, a number of people have contacted me saying they are helping a friend or relative write their story and are not sure if they are going about it in the right way. Here are a few guidelines to help:

- Think carefully before you agree to take on the project. Writing a book for someone else is a huge commitment in time and energy – it is likely to stretch over many months, possibly years.
- You will need to collaborate extensively with the person for whom you are writing the book and interview them so you know them and their story as well as they do.
- Decide at the outset how you will divide up the project. Are you going to share the work or will you be doing it all, including the actual typing of the book?
- Decide at the outset how you will apportion any advance or royalties if the book is published. Professional

ghostwriters usually take 50 per cent of all earnings, but you may be doing it for love. I suggest you have something written down, ideally a contract.

- Gather together all the information you need on the person before you start writing the book.
- Write an outline of the book with a sample chapter and show it to the person you are writing for. This will allow you both to judge if you are going down the right path. Make any necessary adjustments.
- Show the person the text regularly – every two or three chapters – and discuss any changes that need to be made. Collaboration is essential when writing a book with or for someone else and even professional ghostwriters sometimes part company with their clients before the book is finished after falling out. Regular appraisals will keep you on track and mean that you will not waste time by writing something that the other person isn't happy with.

SECTION THREE: PUBLISHING

You have written your work and spent time editing and check-ing it, and you now want to publish your work so that your words will reach a wider audience. You will need to decide if you are going to go down the traditional route of publishing and submit your work to a literary agent or publisher, or, as many now do, try your hand at self-publishing. Or, possibly, you may try the former and then, if you are unable to find an agent or publisher who is interested in your work, decide to self-publish. Self-publishing has never been easier thanks to the internet, but there are pitfalls, which I will come to later. First, let's start by looking at the traditional route of publishing: finding a liter-ary agent who then finds a publisher to publish, market and promote your work.

Agents and Publishers

Many publishers will only consider work submitted through reputable literary agents, because they wouldn't have the time to read the thousands of unsolicited manuscripts they would otherwise receive. Writing is a very popular pastime. Publishers use agents as their front line and rely on their judgement. They will seriously consider any work submitted to them from a reputable agent. However, finding an agent can be as difficult as finding a publisher, as agents are also inundated with enquiries. As I said, writing is a very popular pursuit. My own agent – Andrew Lownie – receives 20,000 submissions a year and signs up a dozen new authors maximum. So how does an unknown author ever become published with so much competition?

Agents earn their living from selling their author's work to publishers (they take a percentage of any advance and royalties). Consequently they are on the lookout for talented new writers whose work is marketable and can be sold to a publisher. If your work is good enough and there is a market for it, eventually you will find an agent who is willing to take you on. Once you have an agent working on your behalf, you stand a much better chance of finding a publisher, as agents know publishers and know which ones will be interested in your work. Having said that, if an agent does sign you up there is no guarantee that your work will be published – you do, however, have the satisfaction of knowing that your work is being taken seriously and that everything is being done to find you a publisher.

Some publishers do still consider unsolicited submissions – that is, work they haven't commissioned an author to write. Also magazines, periodicals, journals and some newspapers accept short stories and articles direct from the writer. If you are thinking of approaching a publisher direct, you will need to research the market to find out which publishers consider unsolicited manuscripts in your genre. This information can be found on their websites and in writers' reference books, such as the *Writers' and Artists' Yearbook*, which is also available online.

Submission Guidelines: General

Here are some dos and don'ts for submitting your work to literary agents and publishers that apply to all genres of writing:

- Follow exactly the agent's or publisher's guidelines for submission. These guidelines can be found on their website or in writers' handbooks. Following them will allow your work to be considered in a highly competitive market. If you don't follow the guidelines then your work is unlikely to be read, as the agent or publisher will have thousands of other submissions to consider – from authors who *have* followed their guidelines.
- Only submit to those agents or publishers who handle your type of work. For example, if an agent handles non-fiction only, it is a waste of your and the agent's time to submit a novel or play. Their areas of expertise will be listed on their website or in the *Writers' and Artists' Yearbook*. My publisher – HarperCollins – for example, is one of the leading publishers of inspirational memoirs.
- Ideally, only submit to one agent or publisher at a time, and to a named person rather than 'Dear Editor' or 'Dear Literary Agent'. Make sure you spell their name correctly. If you do submit to more than one at a time then tell them – it is polite and good practice.

- The covering letter or email that you send with your work is a business letter. Be professional in your approach, as you would if applying for a job.
- If you are posting your material then include a stamped self-addressed envelope (SAE) so that the publisher or agent can return your manuscript if necessary.
- Don't submit your work if the agent or publisher states that they are not accepting any new work at present. There will be good reasons for this and sending your masterpiece won't change their minds – it will just waste everyone's time.
- Don't pester the agent or publisher after you have submitted your work by phoning or emailing. It will take time for them to consider your work. If you haven't received an acknowledgement within two weeks of sending your work then you can follow it up with an email: a polite enquiry asking if they have received your work.

Submission Guidelines: Specific Genres

Articles

You don't need an agent to submit articles to most magazines, newspapers, journals and periodicals; you can submit them directly. These types of publications rely on freelance work to fill their pages, so they make good markets for fledgling writers, and there are plenty of magazines, newspapers and periodicals to choose from. Research your market to find out which publications carry articles similar to the one you have written, or are intending to write, by looking at these publications. Local newspapers often welcome submissions from local writers, especially on community issues. Study the section in the publication for which your article is intended – for example, the business section, the sports page or the women's page, so you know what type of work the editor is looking for.

Submit your article using the publication's submission guidelines. If none are stated then send the following:

- A single-page query letter or email, stating why your article is of interest to the editor.
- Your curriculum vitae, which should include your contact details, website address and publishing history.
- Any photographs relevant to your article.

If you are a fledgling writer then send the article you have written with your query letter and curriculum vitae. If you are a published writer and don't want to write an article that might not be published then you can send the following:

- A query letter.
- Your curriculum vitae, which will include a résumé of past publications.
- A paragraph on how your article will fit into the publication.
- A sample of the proposed article – usually the first two paragraphs.

If you don't receive an acknowledgement after a week, email the editor and ask politely if he or she has received your article. If they say they are considering it, wait. If they are going to publish but want some changes made to the article, thank the editor and make the changes. If they don't make a decision within a month then thank the editor for his or her time and advise them politely that you are submitting your article to another publication. If your piece is rejected, accept the rejection in good humour. Try to build good relationships with the editors – you will be more likely to have your articles published in the future. Most publications pay a small fee for published work, but if you are a new writer the amount won't feel small, as payment sets you firmly in the realms of the professional writer.

Poetry

You do not need an agent to submit poems on your behalf. You can submit them directly to the editor of the publication. Literary journals, periodicals, magazines and some newspapers publish poetry. There are also websites dedicated to publishing poetry online. Some publishers invite poets to submit their work for poetry anthologies they are proposing to publish in the future. You may be asked to buy some of these anthologies in return for having your work published; this is how the publisher recovers their costs and makes a profit. As long as the cost is reasonable, you may be happy to take up this offer.

Research your market thoroughly. Poetry writing is diverse and you will need to familiarize yourself with the type of poem the editor is looking for. This information can be found on the publication's website and in the writers' handbooks. Also look at the poems the editor has previously published; they will want more of the same. Unlike submitting a book, where you are advised to submit to one publisher at a time, you can submit the same poems to more than one publisher. However, if an editor does want to publish your poem then you need to withdraw it from all other editors. Editors like their work to be original and won't be happy to see a piece duplicated in a rival magazine.

Follow the publication's guidelines for submission. If none are stated then submit the following:

- Three or four poems, each on its own page.
- A covering letter, including why your poems may be of interest to the editor.

- Your curriculum vitae, which should include your publishing history.
- A SAE if you are submitting by post, so your work can be returned if necessary.

Keep a record of who has your poems. A spreadsheet with three columns is ideal, showing the title of the poem, where you have submitted it and the result – accepted, or rejected and returned.

Always keep copies of your work. If you don't receive an acknowledgement within two weeks of submitting your poems then send a polite email, asking the editor if your work has been received. If you don't receive a decision in a month, you can reasonably withdraw your work, although there is nothing to be lost in leaving it longer, as it doesn't stop you from submitting your poems elsewhere.

You may consider presenting your poems at poetry readings (see pages 95–6 for advice on promoting your work), in which case it is advisable to have some copies of your work with you so that the audience can purchase them after the reading. If you haven't had your work published then you may consider self-publishing a small, reasonably priced anthology (see section four of this book for advice on self-publishing). Don't become downhearted if you receive lots of rejections. I personally know poets who received hundreds of rejections before they finally had a poem accepted.

Short stories

There is a broad market for short stories and they can be submitted directly to magazines, journals, periodicals and newspapers that publish short stories. You can also enter short-story competitions as well as submit your stories for inclusion in collections and online podcasts. Research your market to see what type of short stories the various publications are looking for. Some magazines are dedicated to short stories but are quite particular about the type of story they want – in content, style and length. Some magazines only publish true-life short stories, for example, so in order to write a story for this market you will need to have experienced something noteworthy in your life that will be of interest to others. Other magazines are dedicated to publishing science fiction, or short stories about true love or crime.

Building an audience for your work through short-story writing is a good way for a fledgling writer to begin. You can expect to be paid for a short story that is published, but there is usually a small fee to enter a writing competition, which is then redistributed as prize money. Publishers of short-story collections who accept your work may ask you to buy a few copies of the book – to recoup their costs and make a profit. You may feel this is an acceptable price for seeing your story in print, providing the cost, quantity and print quality are reasonable.

When submitting a short story, follow the publication's guidelines, which can be found in their entry in the writers' handbooks, on their website or sometimes in the journal itself. If no guidelines are given then send your short story with a covering letter, which should include a very brief synopsis of your story (about fifty words), your curriculum vitae and a SAE for the return of the work if you are submitting by post. Keep copies of your work and keep track of where you have sent your stories. Although competition is fierce, there remains plenty of opportunity for novice short story writers to have their work published.

Books

Research online and in the writers' handbooks which literary agents and publishers handle your type of book, and then follow their guidelines for submission. Regardless of whether you are submitting to a literary agent or directly to a publisher, you will usually need to write a proposal (even though your book may already be written), which you will then send to them. Don't be tempted to send the whole book, unless you are asked to. A well-written proposal can sell your book and is designed to give the agent or publisher all the information they need to decide whether or not they want to see the whole book. Submit your proposal to one agent or publisher at a time and if you don't receive an acknowledgement within two weeks, email a polite enquiry.

A typical proposal will include the following:

Fiction

- A one-page synopsis outlining the plot and narrative structure. Include the word count and, if the novel isn't yet finished, the proposed delivery date.
- A one-page curriculum vitae, including your writing and publishing history.

- A one-page résumé of comparable novels – that is, novels similar to yours that have been published successfully. When listing the books, state their title, author, publisher and date of publication, together with a few lines on how the book compares with yours. Try to choose successful novels, as the agent or publisher is then more likely to look favourably upon yours.
- A one-page résumé of marketing opportunities. You will need to research this. Include marketing outlets such as specialist magazines, websites and organizations. Include your own expertise, and if you have any media presence then include details of that too.
- Brief synopses of each chapter – between half a page and a page for each chapter.
- The first three chapters.

Non-fiction

- A one-page synopsis showing what makes the book fresh and exciting. Include the word count and, if the book isn't yet finished, the proposed delivery date.
- A one-page curriculum vitae, including your writing and publishing history, and why you are qualified to write the book.
- A one-page résumé of comparable books – that is, books similar to yours that have been published successfully in recent years. When listing the books, give their title, author, publisher and date of publication, together with a few lines on how the book compares with yours.

- One page listing the sources you used to write your book, similar to the bibliography you find at the end of a non-fiction book.
- A one-page résumé of marketing opportunities, which you will need to research. Include marketing outlets such as specialist magazines, websites and organizations. Include your own expertise, and if you have any media presence then include details of that here too.
- Brief synopses of each chapter – between half a page and a page for each chapter.
- A sample chapter and, if appropriate, a few relevant photographs.

Writing a proposal is not as complex as it may sound – I have included a sample of one at the end of this book (see page 111). Use the usual Arial, 12-point font on A4-size paper, and don't forget to paginate the proposal as a separate document. If you are submitting by email, send the proposal as an attachment, unless instructed otherwise by the agent or publisher. If you are submitting by post then staple or paperclip the proposal as a separate document, and include a brief covering letter. Obviously keep a copy of your proposal just as you do the actual book, as you will want to resubmit it if the first agent or publisher doesn't make you an offer. Writing a proposal may seem like a lot of extra work, especially if your book is already written, but proposals sell books, so it is worth putting the same effort into writing your proposal as you put into the actual book.

Plays

Literary agents and publishers who accept plays are listed in writers' handbooks and online. It is a specialist market; not as many agents and publishers handle plays as they do books. However, some agencies and publishers do specialize in plays and some websites are dedicated to publishing them. Plays accepted by the editors of these websites are uploaded so that theatre groups, schools and colleges can browse through them and hopefully buy. Given the diversity of play formats – including screenplays, short one-act plays, musicals, comedies and adult and children's plays, to name a few – you need to research your market thoroughly. Not all agencies and publishers that accept plays accept all types of plays.

Once you have found an agent or publisher who handles your type of play, follow their guidelines for submission, which will be included in their entry in writers' handbooks or on their website. In the first instance, you may be asked to send a synopsis of your play, including the title, word count, storyline, characters, target audience and details of any music, together with a covering letter or email and your curriculum vitae. If the agent or publisher is interested, they will ask to see the whole play. Unless instructed otherwise, use the format for the play as outlined on pages 64–73 of this book and submit as an email attachment. Never submit an incomplete or half-finished play. You can submit your play to more than one agent or publisher at a time, but if you receive an offer then notify any other agents or publishers who are still considering your work.

Children's books

Children's books are another specialist market, and not all agents and publishers who accept children's books accept all age ranges of children's books. Some, for example, don't handle picture books but will consider books for older children. Agents and publishers that accept children's books, and the age ranges they accept, will be listed in writers' handbooks and on their websites. Follow the agent's or publisher's guidelines for submission. This will usually include the following:

- A covering letter or email.
- Your curriculum vitae, including your publishing history.
- A one-page synopsis of the book, including the plot, genre and the age group for which the book is intended.
- The whole of the book, if it is a picture book.
- An extract – usually the first two chapters, if it is a longer book.
- A half-page synopsis of each chapter.
- A SAE, if you are submitting by post.

You can submit children's books to more than one agent or publisher at a time, but once someone shows an interest, withdraw it from the others. Keep copies of your work and do not send original artwork until it is asked for – and then send it by a very safe and reliable method, so it doesn't go astray in the post.

Promoting Your Book

Much to your delight your book is going to be published, so now you need to help your publisher promote your work. Although your publisher will take care of the distribution of your book – that is, getting it into shops, supermarkets and available to buy online – you will be expected to play your part in promotion to help sell it. Do whatever the public relations department of your publisher asks you to do (within reason): attend the book signings, tours, interviews and talks they may organize for you. Also, arrange some yourself, assuming you are not writing under a pseudonym for confidentiality reasons and have to protect your anonymity. If you've written a children's book, ask schools if you can give groups of children a talk about your work. Take in some signed copies of your book that can be purchased by the school or the pupils. Make sure your talk is age appropriate for your target audience and has an educational value.

Your publisher will give you some complimentary copies of your book and you will probably want to give some of these to your family, friends and work colleagues. Ask them to spread news of your book by reviewing it online. You could also give copies to anyone who might be influential in promoting your book, at clubs or organizations you belong to, for example. Any extra copies can be given to charities for charity auctions. Once you're an established author, you will receive plenty of emails from charities asking if you can donate a signed copy of your book for a charity auction. Not only does this raise money for a good cause, but it will help to promote your book.

As a published author you will need a website on which to advertise your books, tell your readers a bit about yourself and keep them up to date with what is going on. A blog is a good way of doing this. Your publisher may help you set up a website, or there are many companies who will design and host a website for you. Costs vary, so shop around. The higher your online presence the better, so join social-networking websites, such as Facebook and Twitter, and work on building up a fan base.

Join online writing communities and book groups, but don't just post about your book – join in the discussion about other books too. Review other authors' works kindly – never be tempted to rubbish a competitor; there is enough room in the market for everyone. Create an author profile on Amazon and similar bookselling websites; readers like to know about their authors. You can do this even if you are writing under a pseudonym, but obviously don't include a photograph or any identifying details of yourself. You could use the book cover for the image instead.

SECTION FOUR: SELF-PUBLISHING

Whether you are a novelist, diarist, poet, playwright or the author of non-fiction or children's books, you can self-publish your work. With the advances in technology self-publishing has never been easier, more accessible or more affordable. However, self-publishing is not a new idea and many now-famous authors originally self-published their work: for example, Beatrix Potter, D. H. Lawrence, Oscar Wilde, Edgar Allan Poe, Ernest Hemingway and John Grisham, to name a few.

Authors self-publish for a number of reasons, but often it is because they can't interest an agent or publisher in their work. Self-publishing may therefore seem like the writer's dream, especially if you have spent years submitting your book to publishers and agents only to have it rejected over and over again. However, there are pitfalls as well as advantages to self-publishing. I dabbled in self-publishing with a novel a few years ago, so I have some experience and know first hand the work that needs to go into a self-publishing project in order to produce a book to a high standard.

So what are the advantages and disadvantages of going it alone and self-publishing?

Advantages:
- You will have the satisfaction of finally seeing your work in print.
- All the money you make will be yours – apart from your costs.
- You will retain full control over the publishing process and copyright.
- Your book may be spotted and taken up by a mainstream publisher.

Disadvantages:
- You will need to employ the services of an editor or proofreader if your book is to be of a professional standard.
- You will have to commit a lot of time and energy to the project. Be prepared for a steep learning curve.
- The quality of self-published books varies, in both printed books and e-books, and you will be responsible for quality control.
- Many reviewers will not review a self-published book.
- You will struggle to get your books into shops and supermarkets.
- Marketing, distributing and promoting your work effectively will be difficult, very time consuming, and also expensive if you employ a distributor and PR firm to do it for you.

If you want to self-publish and see your book in print, you will not be deterred by the disadvantages, so let's look at the process of self-publishing. The first step is to check that your work is without error. I would recommend using an editor, or at least a proofreader. If your book goes out littered with mistakes, consumers will not only lose confidence in your work but in self-published work in general. Details of freelance editors and proofreaders can be found online, in writers' handbooks and journals. Check that all your pages are in the correct order, including the title page, the acknowledgements page, contents page and index, if applicable, and then paginate from the first page of chapter one. You will also need to decide on a cover for your book. If you are not artistic then I suggest you use a design firm that offers book jacket services. They can be found online and are relatively inexpensive considering the enormity of what they are delivering. The book cover is probably the single most important factor in your book (apart from your writing) – a good book jacket will help sell your book.

You will also need to be clear of any legal ramifications that might result from your book. This is especially important if it is a memoir, biography, diary or any true-life story where others may be implicated or identified – either named or anonymized. Publishing houses have their own legal team who thoroughly check all books – including fiction – before they are published, thereby minimizing the risk of being sued. If you self-publish, assessing the legal repercussions will be your responsibility. If you have any doubts, pay for a legal report. They are not cheap, but it will be cheaper than being sued. The Society of Authors carries a list of solicitors offering this service, as does the Law Society, Chambers and Partners, and other online websites.

So, now your book has been thoroughly checked and edited, and you have decided on a cover, you are ready to self-publish. There are three main ways of self-publishing your work: use a small independent press; use an online print-on-demand service (POD); produce an e-book. First, you will need to apply for an ISBN (International Standard Book Number) in the country in which you are publishing. This is a unique reference number that identifies your book. In the UK you purchase these in blocks of ten, so you will either have excess or some in hand for future books you may self-publish. The ISBN will need to be shown on your book.

Independent Presses

Employing a small independent press to print a book or anthology of poems was the method self-publishers used before the advent of publishing on the internet. This method still has relevance today. These firms are small independent companies who will print your book for you – exactly as you want it, and as many copies as you want. Some of these firms have developed into small independent publishers so that, as well as printing your book, they include some marketing and distribution, and will also advise you on the publication process. But beware of new start-up companies, of which there are many on the internet. Use a well-established firm; their details can be found online, in writers' reference books and journals and in trade magazines.

Before you sign a contract with an independent press or publisher, check the quality of their books. Reputable independent presses will show you samples of their work. Check the quality of the paper, ink and book jacket. There are usually different qualities to choose from and the better quality the more it will cost you to print. A reputable firm will also print a single copy of your book first to make sure you are happy with it before they print the whole order. You will need to decide on the font style and size, and a good small press will advise you. You will also need to cost your book and decide on the price to charge. This may depend on how many copies you order (known as the print run). Usually the more copies you order the cheaper per copy your book will be to print (due to 'economies of scale'). However, many small presses are now using print-on-demand (POD) technology so that, while the unit price of the book will be higher, it is not affected by the number ordered. Be realistic in the number of copies you have printed. Not only will you have to pay for the books, you will need to store and sell them, so don't get carried away. I would suggest that, if you are publishing a first book, and you don't have orders for more, an initial print run of 500 copies is plenty. Don't forget to include the ISBN and price on your book, and if you have a website, which I would strongly advise you do, then include the website address too.

Print on Demand (POD)

Print on demand, or POD as it is known, is internet-based publishing where, as its name suggests, books are printed on demand – that is, only when an order is placed and paid for. POD has revolutionized self-publishing and brought the process within reach of most authors.

Advantages of POD:
- Self-publishers don't have to buy books up front.
- It is relatively inexpensive to publish a POD book.
- Once uploaded, a book need never go out of print.
- The book has a worldwide platform and is available to anyone who has access to a computer and a postal system which can deliver the book to them.

Disadvantages of POD:
- You will be responsible for all aspects of the book's production.
- The retail price of a POD book is usually higher than those produced by traditional print runs, because there is no economy of scale: each book has to be treated as if it is the only one sold. The higher price becomes more significant when set alongside the thousands of heavily discounted books that are now available online.

- The quality of the paper, ink and book jacket of POD books varies, so it is important to see a sample book before you sign up.
- As with any self-published book, the standard of the content relies heavily on the integrity of the author, so use an editor or proofreader.
- Some POD books are a great disappointment and simply not worth the money, which diminishes consumer confidence in self-publishing in general.

Shop around for a POD publisher – there are many online. Choose well-established companies with a good track record. Compare their terms and conditions and read their contract carefully. How long are you signed up for? Who retains the copyright? How much is their postage and packing? How is the money from book sales collected and how does it reach you? All this information should be easily accessible and transparent. Check where the POD publisher's website appears on search engines and where they will market your book. High-ranking websites are crucial, as selling a POD book relies on customers finding your book on the internet.

Once you have decided on your POD publisher, you will need to upload your book onto their website. Step-by-step instructions on how to do this will be found on the POD publisher's website. However, there are companies who offer a complete package and will edit, proofread and upload your POD book, and also market it online, for a cost. You may be able to pick and choose which part of the package you want. Once your book is available online, the public can purchase it as they would any other book online; there is nothing to show that it is a POD book.

E-books

E-book is short for electronic book, also known as a digital book. These are books published in digital format; that is, they are not printed on paper. An e-book has to be published on the internet, through one of the many digital publishing platforms that are now available. The e-book is then bought online and downloaded by the reader onto an e-book reader, computer, tablet, smartphone or similar electronic device.

In the last few years e-books have gained popularity, and sales at present account for approximately half of all book sales. Mainstream publishers now publish most of their books in e-book format as well as paperback and (less often) hardback, to cover both markets. Many self-publishers have seized upon the relative ease of e-book publishing and, avoiding the costs of publishing a physical book, have published in e-book format only. While there are clear advantages to this strategy – cost, speed and ease of publication and instant access to a worldwide market – publishing in e-book only immediately halves your potential market. Some self-publishers have begun by publishing in e-book format and then, spurred on by their success, have also published a physical book by POD or using a small print run (see page 102).

Although publishing an e-book is relatively easy and inexpensive, there are hurdles to overcome and pitfalls to avoid. A first-time self-publisher who goes it alone is likely to be on a steep learning curve. To begin with, there are many different e-book formats in use. I counted twenty-seven recently, which included the eight main formats used. Many of these different digital formats are not compatible with each other, so one e-book format cannot necessarily be downloaded and read on all devices. In order to reach your widest audience, your e-book will need to be produced in all the main formats. If you are technically minded, you may be able to make these conversions yourself. If not, there are many companies online who (for a fee) will convert your e-book into the main formats and will also upload it for you onto the various platforms. Shop around online and choose an established company with a good track record and whose costs for conversion and uploading are reasonable. Check their terms and conditions to make sure you retain ownership of your e-book.

Some e-book publishers and digital platforms that sell e-books require the books to have ISBNs; others do not. To maximize your distribution potential, it is advisable to give your book an ISBN (see page 100). Some e-book publishing companies will acquire the ISBN for you, but if they do then technically they become your publisher, so read the terms and conditions in their contract.

You will need a good cover for your e-book, just as you do for a physical book, and one that can be viewed successfully on all e-readers, large and small and with high- and low-resolution screens. If you feel out of your depth designing a suitable book cover that satisfies these requirements then it is advisable to use the services of an e-book graphic designer – there are many online. Shop around and look at the galleries of their work, which will be displayed on their websites. Check their costs and phone them to discuss ideas for your cover. It shouldn't be expensive to produce an interesting and original e-book cover – under £100 – and it is important for your e-book to look good, as it will help boost sales.

Don't forget to include all the additional pages in your e-book, just as you would in a physical book: title page, acknowledgements, contents, index of searchable terms, copyright page, etc. Price your e-book competitively, but don't give it away as some authors do so that it rises up the e-book charts. You've put a lot of work into your book and if you give it away you will be devaluing not only this book, but also any future books – your readers will expect them for nothing. Price your book competitively and then promote it. The success of your e-book will depend largely on what you do to promote and market it and there is plenty you can do.

Distribution, Marketing and Promotion

Once you have self-published your book you will have to market and sell it, and you can't afford to be shy about this. You will need to be very proactive when distributing and marketing your book, and put yourself forward – as a self-published author all this will be your responsibility. If you have a physical book – that is, from a print run or POD – there are firms that offer distribution, marketing and PR services for self-published authors, and their details can be found online or in writers' handbooks and journals. They are not cheap, however, and using their services will add to your costs considerably. Most self-publishers do their own distribution, marketing and PR, and this is how:

- Take copies of your book or anthology with you wherever you go and sell them to your family, friends, work colleagues, and at any clubs or organizations you belong to – in fact, sell them to anyone who knows you. You will find that family and friends will be interested in your self-publishing venture and will oblige you by buying a copy. If you've written a children's book, ask schools if you can give groups of children talks about your work and thereby promote your book. Schools are used to having visiting authors and will often oblige, providing there is an educational value to your talk.

- Approach your local bookshops and small independent stores that sell books and magazines and ask them if they will stock some of your books on a sale-or-return basis. Local shops are often happy to display books by local authors and may even arrange a book signing for you. You may need to think about display and possibly provide a small display stand so that the shop can showcase your books. Approach independent bookshops in other parts of the country; they are more likely to take your books than a large chain store is. Sell your books from your website (adding the cost of postage and packing) and from other reputable bookselling websites, such as Amazon, The Book Depository and Play.com. Create an author profile on these websites and blog about matters of interest. Use your website to update readers and create a good relationship with them.

- Contact (by letter or email) the editors of magazines, newspapers and websites that review books or have previously carried articles similar in subject matter to that of your book and ask if they would be willing to review a copy of your book. Send a copy immediately if they are interested. Mainstream publishers send out dozens of review copies of new books on spec to editors of leading magazines, but they have the resources to do this; as a self-published author with limited funds, I suggest you send a short letter or email first and then follow it up with the book if they are interested. Send copies of your book with a short covering letter to the editors of local newspapers. They are usually happy to review a book by a local author and may possibly interview you too.

- Arrange talks and readings in libraries, arts venues, groups, clubs and organizations to promote and sell your book. However, if you are writing under a pseudonym and need to protect your anonymity for reasons of confidentiality, you won't be able to promote your book in person and will have to market and sell from a distance, so make full use of the internet. Join social-networking websites, such as Facebook and Twitter. Blog and join online writing communities and book groups, but don't just write about your book – join in the discussion about other books too, and review kindly other authors' works. If you have published in e-book only, then the majority of your marketing and PR will be done on the internet, but there is nothing stopping you from promoting your book in person by giving talks and readings. Print some attractive flyers promoting your book, including the URL of the website where it can be downloaded, and hand them out at the end of your talk or reading. As a self-published author, the success of your book is entirely down to you, so be inventive and think of new ways to market and promote your book so that it stands out against the thousands of others.

Good luck with your writing and publishing. I look forward to reading your book. Most importantly, enjoy your writing. Write from your soul and you won't be disappointed.

SAMPLE PROPOSAL

Title Page

[Title of Work]
By
[Author's Name]
Represented by:
[Your agent's name and address]

(If you don't have an agent, include your own contact details.)

Contents

Synopsis (from my proposal for *Happy Kids*)

Happy Kids by Cathy Glass is a self-help guide for successfully managing children's behaviour – from babies to young adults. Her technique, called 'The 3Rs', is her own, and is based on sound child-management strategies. The book is 65,800 words and is ready for submission.

A brief introduction explains Cathy's background and experience, the premise for the book and her '3Rs' technique for managing children's behaviour. The book approaches child-development chronologically, giving detailed and easy-to-follow advice on managing children's behaviour during the various stages of development, beginning with settling a baby quickly into a routine.

Happy Kids focuses on children's behaviour, and Cathy draws on her vast experience of managing and improving children's unacceptable behaviour by describing practical examples of how the 3Rs works. Addressing issues such as smacking (don't), shouting and aggression, Cathy explains why children misbehave and what parents can do to change their children's bad behaviour.

Although the book is primarily aimed at parents, the techniques can be successfully used by other professionals working in the field of childcare. There is a chapter dedicated to teachers, and another to nannies, nursery nurses and childminders, showing strategies for managing individual and group behaviour. Three chapters deal with children who are out of control, where a step-by-step plan shows the parents how to 'turn around' a difficult child.

Another chapter explains sibling rivalry, what parents can do to avoid this and how to improve unacceptable sibling behaviour. The effect of diet on behaviour is highly topical, and the book quotes scientific research explaining the effect of food additives on behaviour and the importance of vitamins and Omega 3 oil.

With schools now having upwards of 20 per cent of their pupils diagnosed as special needs, another chapter addresses behaviour in respect of special needs: autism, ADHD, bipolar and other behavioural disorders. Cathy shows that using the 3Rs approach can dramatically improve behaviour, even in children with a diagnosed 'condition'.

The book begins with the newborn baby, and the penultimate chapter is dedicated to young adults – even at twenty, 'children' still need guidelines and advice on acceptable behaviour. The book closes with a summary, highlighting the techniques and strategies for raising confident and well-behaved children who are a credit to their parents and society.

Competing Literature (from my proposal for *Happy Adults*)

At present there are no books on the market exactly like *Happy Adults*. However, the book's obvious similarities to other successful titles suggest the book's considerable commercial potential.

Self-help guides continue to dominate the bestseller market worldwide, with recent UK and European bestsellers including: *Control Stress: Stop Worrying and Feel Good Now* (Paul McKenna, Bantam Press, 2009), teaching techniques for managing stress; *The Secret* (Rhonda Byrne, Simon & Schuster Ltd, 2006), in which the author shares the secret for achieving everything we desire; *59 Seconds: Think a Little, Change a Lot* (Richard Wiseman, Macmillan, 2009), containing quick strategies to help us achieve our aims and ambitions; *The Power of Now* (Eckhart Tolle, Mobius, 2001) – how to find happiness and enlightenment by living in the here and now; and, of course, Dale Carnegie's classic guide on making the most of life, *How to Win Friends and Influence People* – originally published by Simon & Schuster Ltd in 1936 and still popular over seventy-five years later.

Many self-help books in the United States have become modern-day classics and are still in the bestseller charts over 10 years after publication: *The Seven Habits of Highly Effective People* (Steven Covey, Simon & Schuster Ltd, 1999) – 15 million copies sold; *Chicken Soup for the Soul* (Vermilion, new edition, 2000), now part of a highly successful series; *Awaken the Giant Within* (Anthony Robbins, Pocket Books, new edition, 2001) – guidelines for using thoughts and emotions to attain goals, with over 3 million copies sold; *Don't Sweat the Small Stuff* (Richard Carlson, Mobius, 1996), containing advice on how to do what matters most, now part of a series and still popular fifteen years after publication!

The popularity of self-help books shows no sign of waning. A recent article in *Psychology Today* stated that there are now more self-help books in print than there are cookbooks. Each year we purchase millions of books to make ourselves slimmer, calmer, smarter, richer, more confident and more attractive. *Happy Adults* brings together all these components for a happier and contented lifestyle.

The popularity of these books is cross-cultural and international. The *Beijing Times* recently reported that Chinese bookstores have been 'swamped' with books on self-awareness and how to deal with loss and misfortune, while Fatima Mernisi's books have found broad popularity beyond her native Morocco. An article from Tehran, reported in the *Pittsburgh Post-Gazette*, stated that 'self-help books are the hottest items at the busy line of bookstores along the campus of Tehran University'.

Although diverse in technique, self-help books have the following in common: they present themselves in optimistic terms; they speak directly to the reader in clear language; they help the reader live a fuller life. *Happy Adults* fulfils all the criteria, as well as developing the genre with a fresh and exciting perspective.

Marketing Outlets (using my book *Happy Kids*, here is an example for non-fiction)

Happy Kids by Cathy Glass has wide commercial appeal with a huge target audience of parents, carers, teachers, nursery nurses, nannies, childminders; in fact, anyone who looks after children and is responsible for children's behaviour.

Happy Kids was spawned by the success of Cathy Glass's eleven fostering memoirs published by HarperElement. These books not only depicted the dreadful lives of the children Cathy fostered before they came into care, but also showed her successfully managing and improving the children's often very challenging behaviour. *Happy Kids* will fit well into the proposed publishing schedule and complement past and future memoirs.

Parenting guides are hugely popular, as anxious parents search for ways to help raise their children in societies where children are often seen as anti-social and aggressive. There are many guides on raising children, but none quite like *Happy Kids*, which deals specifically with behaviour and shows how to change it for the better with clear, practical advice.

There are numerous outlets for this book, with the potential for reaching millions of parents and professionals. Supermarkets dedicate extensive shelf-space to parenting guides, as do mainstream bookshops. Various parenting magazines carry adverts and feature articles for books: *Mother & Baby*; *Pregnancy & Birth*; *Parent & Child*; *Parents*; *Family Fun*; *Family Circle*, etc. There are over 260,000 websites for parents, with online communities, discussion boards and links to books and author interviews; for example, www.mumsnet.com and www.netmums.com.

Foster Care magazine, *Who Cares?*, *Children Now*, *Young People Now* and *Community Care* are monthly magazines for those working with, or caring for, children; they have joint circulation in excess of 200,000. Some of these magazines have already (positively) reviewed Cathy's books and carried question-and-answer interviews with her. There is the potential for extending this into a column, which is being investigated.

The Times Educational Supplement, weekly circulation of 85,000, goes into all schools and mainstream newsagents. It carries adverts, editorials and advice on all aspects of managing children, including much discussion on behaviour. Nursery nurses, nannies and childminders are catered for through weekly journals – *Child Care*; *Nursery World*; *The Register*; *Early Years Educator* – as well as online magazines, such as www.childrenwebmag.com; all of which carry advertisements for books, book extracts, author interviews and advice for managing children.

Marketing Outlets (using my book *Run, Mummy, Run*, here is an example for fiction)

Run, Mummy, Run is a mainstream novel with wide commercial appeal. Psychological dramas depicting domestic violence continue to be popular. *Sleeping with the Enemy* by Nancy Price (Arrow, 1988) remains in print, and was a major film starring Julia Roberts. Likewise Joy Fielding's *See Jane Run* (Headline 1991) and *Don't Cry Now* (Headline 1995) have fed the reading public's appetite for this type of literature. *Run, Mummy, Run* takes the subject of domestic violence into the twenty-first century by reflecting our multicultural society; the victim is Asian and is married to Mark who is white.

Literature reflecting our multicultural society has become increasingly popular, both in the UK and US. These books no longer simply accommodate 'ethnic minorities' and are hugely popular with the reading public at large. *The Color Purple* by Alice Walker (now a Women's Press Classic, 2001) and Hanif Kureishi's *The Buddha of Suburbia* (Faber & Faber, 1991) brought this writing to the attention of the mainstream reading public. The script of Kureishi's hugely successful television drama *My Beautiful Launderette* still sells well (Faber, 2000). Current literature driving this popular market includes Zadie Smith's greatly acclaimed *White Teeth* (Hamish Hamilton, 2000) and Monica Ali's *Brick Lane* (Black Swan, 2004). *Run, Mummy, Run* will appeal to a large cross-cultural audience.

The subject matter of this book, domestic violence, remains highly topical and present in the public arena. In the US a staggering 43 per cent of women are physically, verbally or emotionally abused. Every nine seconds a woman is physically assaulted by her husband, and 30 per cent of injured women attending A&E are victims of 'wife battering'. Similar figures are reflected in the UK. Statistics for Asian women are even higher, but domestic violence remains a taboo subject in the culture and goes largely unreported. Jasvinder Sanghera's poignant memoir *Shame* (Hodder & Stoughton, 2007) shows what can happen in an Asian family when domestic violence is ignored. *Run, Mummy, Run* is therefore likely to spark debate and appeal to Radio 4's *Open Book*, *Book at Bedtime* and *The Afternoon Reading*.

Run, Mummy, Run is 90,000 words long and the manuscript is ready for submission. The strong, direct style and episodic narrative, which are characteristic of Cathy Glass's writing, would adapt easily and successfully to a play for television or even a film.

Character Summaries (from my novel *Run, Mummy, Run*)

(You may be asked to include character summaries in a proposal for fiction.)

Main characters

Aisha is an attractive, intelligent and hard-working Asian woman. Although she was born in England and is Westernized, she respects and adheres to her parents' traditional (and strict) views. As a result, she leads a sheltered life and is naïve in many respects. When she finds herself trapped in a highly abusive marriage, she hasn't the resources to deal with it and cannot confide in her parents for fear of bringing shame on them.

Mark is ten years older than Aisha, successful, confident and very worldly wise. He enjoys the good things in life and is particularly proud of his BMW, which he changes every year. Mark appears charming and can convincingly explain why the breakdowns of his two previous marriages were not his fault. He is good at controlling people without them realizing it, and controls Aisha by persuading her he is acting in her best interest. Once Mark has Aisha where he wants her – at home with a baby and entirely dependent on him – he controls her through fear and mental and physical abuse.

Minor characters

Belinda owns the dating agency Aisha turns to in order to find herself a partner. Belinda is very sophisticated, successful and fashionable. Her agency is exclusive and she prides herself on personally vetting all her clients. Belinda is very good at her job and very persuasive. Any doubts Aisha entertains about Mark are easily swept away by Belinda. Later, when Aisha has lost everything, she blames Belinda for the clever way she packaged Mark for sale.

Aisha's parents are from Gujarat and have retained many of their traditional values. Aisha's father is proud of what he has achieved in England and holds himself up as an example for Aisha to follow. It is pride and family honour that keep Aisha trapped in a violent and loveless marriage. Aisha's mother always wears a sari, having never got used to Western clothes. She is the traditional Asian wife. She would never question her husband's views, and has never worked outside of the home. At the end, when her husband has mellowed through age, she becomes more assertive.

Sarah and James are Aisha and Mark's children and they live in fear of their father's violence. They have never seen their father show kindness towards their mother. They are seven and five respectively when the majority of the action takes places. At seven, Sarah is very mature and protective of her younger brother, James. She looks after her mother when she has been assaulted by her father. The children instinctively know their home is not one they can bring their friends to.

Tony is Mark's driver at work and brings Aisha home from the hospital after the birth of Sarah when Mark has been delayed. Tony is a kind and caring family man and the antithesis of Mark. Tony sets the scene before Mark's first horrendous attack on Aisha.

Christine was Mark's second wife who, according to Mark, was a violent alcoholic. Aisha doesn't meet her until the end, when she goes looking for her, believing she is still seeing Mark. The person Aisha finds is very different from the one Mark has portrayed. Christine tells Aisha that history has repeated itself and that she suffered at the hands of Mark, just as Aisha has done. It is hearing this that starts Aisha along the path to recovery.

About the Author (this will be your curriculum vitae)

Cathy Glass

Cathy is an international bestselling author and a foster carer. She has written eighteen books, including eleven fostering memoirs, four self-help guides and three novels. All Cathy's memoirs have been top-ten bestsellers, with *Damaged* (HarperElement, 2007) staying at number one in the *Sunday Times* bestseller list for over three months and listed the number-one e-book in the *New York Times*.

Cathy's books are published in seven languages as well as in large-print editions. To date, her books have sold over 1.4 million copies worldwide and film rights are being explored. Recent publications include *Happy Mealtimes for Kids*, *Please Don't Take My Baby* and *Will You Love Me?*

Cathy has always combined writing with fostering, rising very early in the morning to write before the day begins with her ever-changing family. Prior to the publication of *Damaged*, she had written short stories, articles and poems for various national magazines and newspapers. As well as having wide mainstream appeal, her books are used by lecturers, trainers and practitioners working in social care, childcare and education.

Cathy Glass is a pseudonym and, while Cathy needs to maintain her anonymity, this has not detracted from her popularity. Cathy appears on most popular networking sites, including Facebook and Twitter.

Cathy has her own popular website (25,000-plus hits per day) – www.cathyglass.co.uk – which includes:

Details of her published books and links to order.

Forthcoming titles with links to pre-order.

Articles written by her, and Q&A interviews.

Comments from readers who are encouraged to email.

A blog by Cathy, which includes her personal views on topical issues.

A Happy Kids Forum where Cathy answers readers' childcare questions.

A contact page so that readers can email Cathy personally.

Cathy replies to as many emails as time allows and readers are very pleased to receive this personal response. She also emails readers when a new book is due out. As a result of Cathy's personal touch, she has built up a loyal, international and growing readership of committed fans who recommend her books to others.

Chapter Summaries (an example of one chapter summary from my proposal for *Hidden*)

(Include a half- to full-page summary per chapter of all the chapters in your book, unless the agent or publisher instructs otherwise.)

CHAPTER THREE

Tayo still hadn't arrived by 3 p.m. and I wondered what had happened as his school was only twenty minutes away. The waiting was setting my nerves on edge, as I was sure it was for Tayo, particularly after being taken from school by the police. It wasn't the best way to start a placement. Brian, the social worker, phoned and said he had stopped off at the social services offices and would be with me shortly.

When Tayo arrived he was very different from the distressed child that I had imagined. He was calm, confident, intelligent, very well spoken and had impeccable good manners. He wasn't at all like any child I'd fostered before. Clearly at some point Tayo must have had some very good parenting; however, he had a poor self-image when it came to his racial identity. Tayo asked me if all my family was white like he was. Tayo was in fact mixed race.

The Essential Information forms Brian gave me were all blank, because there were still no details about Tayo. Tayo didn't even have any medical records, because he'd never seen a doctor since he'd been in this country. I asked Tayo how long that was and he said five years. I was shocked.

When Brian left, I showed Tayo around and introduced him to my teenage children. Tayo had arrived with only what he stood up in, and when I asked him if he knew where all his belongings were he wouldn't answer. I knew it would be a long time before he trusted me enough to confide in me.

Sample Chapter(s)

[Your sample chapter(s)]

(This can be just one chapter or as many as three, so writers should follow the agent's or publisher's guidelines.)

Useful Resources

The Society of Authors

Protects the interests of authors and offers lots of useful advice. You are eligible to join as soon as you have been offered a publishing contract.

Contact: The Society of Authors, 84 Drayton Gardens, London, SW10 9SB
Website: www.societyofauthors.net
Email: info@societyofauthors.org
Telephone: 020 7373 6643

Public Lending Remuneration (PLR)

Register your details with them as soon as you have a book published so you receive payment for books borrowed from public libraries.

Contact: Public Lending Right, First Floor, Richard House, Sorbonne Close, Stockton-on-Tees, TS17 6DA
Website: www.plr.uk.com, including online registration.
Telephone: 01642 604699

The Authors' Licensing and Collecting Society (ALCS)

Register when you have a book published to receive secondary royalties.

Contact: ALCS, The Writers' House, 13 Haydon Street, London, EC3N 1DB

Website: www.alcs.co.uk, including online registration.

Email: alcs@alcs.co.uk

Telephone: 020 7264 5700

Writers' and Artists' Yearbook

Advice and information for writers of all genres. Includes details of publishers, literary agents, magazines, newspapers, writing competitions, prizes and editorial services.

Book and website: www.writersandartists.co.uk

Cathy Glass

———

One remarkable woman, more
than **100** foster children cared for.

Learn more about the many
lives Cathy has touched.

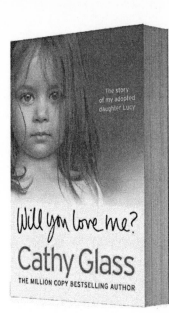

Will You Love Me?

A broken child desperate for a loving home

The true story of Cathy's adopted daughter Lucy.

Please Don't Take My Baby

Seventeen-year-old Jade is pregnant, homeless and alone

Cathy has room in her heart for two.

Another Forgotten Child

Eight-year-old Aimee was on the child-protection register at birth

Cathy is determined to give her the happy home she deserves.

A Baby's Cry

A newborn, only hours old, taken into care

Cathy protects tiny Harrison from the potentially fatal secrets that surround his existence.

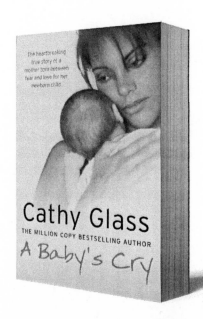

The Night the Angels Came

A little boy on the brink of bereavement

Cathy and her family make sure Michael is never alone.

Mummy Told Me Not to Tell

A troubled boy sworn to secrecy

After his dark past has been revealed, Cathy helps Reece to rebuild his life.

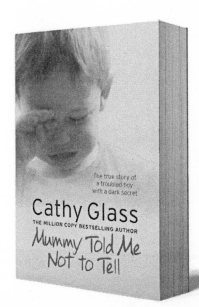

I Miss Mummy

Four-year-old Alice doesn't understand why she's in care

Cathy fights for her to have the happy home she deserves.

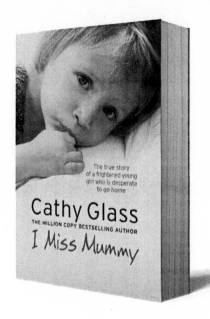

The Saddest Girl in the World

A haunted child who refuses to speak

Do Donna's scars run too deep for Cathy to help?

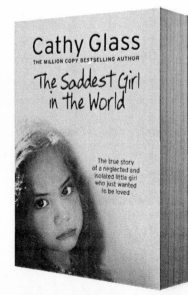

Cut

Dawn is desperate to be loved

Abused and abandoned, this vulnerable child pushes Cathy and her family to their limits.

Hidden

The boy with no past

Can Cathy help Tayo to feel like he belongs again?

Damaged

A forgotten child

Cathy is Jodie's last hope. For the first time, this abused young girl has found someone she can trust.

Fiction inspired by true stories...

Run, Mummy, Run

The gripping story of a woman caught in a horrific cycle of abuse, and the desperate measures she must take to escape.

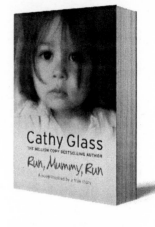

My Dad's a Policeman

The dramatic short story about a young boy's desperate bid to keep his family together.

The Girl in the Mirror

Trying to piece together her past, Mandy uncovers a dreadful family secret that has been blanked from her memory for years.

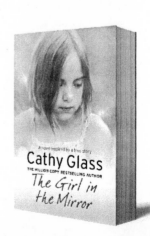

Sharing her expertise...

Happy Kids

A clear and concise guide to raising confident, well-behaved and happy children.

Happy Adults

A practical guide to achieving lasting happiness, contentment and success. The essential manual for getting the best out of life.

Happy Mealtimes for Kids

A guide to healthy eating with simple recipes that children love.

Be amazed
Be moved
Be inspired

———

Discover more about Cathy Glass
visit www.cathyglass.co.uk

Printed by RR Donnelley at Glasgow, UK